LUCRETIUS

LUCRETIUS

HIS CONTINUING INFLUENCE
AND
CONTEMPORARY RELEVANCE

edited by
Timothy J. Madigan
and
David B. Suits

RIT PRESS

2011

Lucretius: His Continuing Influence and Contemporary Relevance
Edited by Timothy J. Madigan and David B. Suits

Published and distributed by
RIT Press
90 Lomb Memorial Drive
Rochester, New York 14623-5604
http://carypress.rit.edu

Inquiries about the content of this publication may be directed to the editors in care of
Department of Philosophy
College of Liberal Arts
Rochester Institute of Technology
92 Lomb Memorial Drive
Rochester, New York 14623

Printed in the U.S.
ISBN 978-1-933360-49-2

Cover image: Spencer Arnold/Stringer / Hulton Archive / Getty Images
Cover text: *Titi Lucretii Cari de rerum natura. Libri sex.* Birmingham, Eng.: John Baskerville, 1773.

Library of Congress Cataloging-in-Publication Data

Lucretius : his continuing influence and contemporary relevance / edited by Timothy J. Madigan
and David B. Suits.
    p. cm.
  Papers from a conference held in March 2009 at St. John Fisher College, Rochester, N.Y.
  Includes bibliographical references and index.
  1. Lucretius Carus, Titus--Congresses. I. Madigan, Timothy J. II. Suits, David B.
  B577.L64L76 2011
  187—dc22

                        2011000772

LUCRETIUS:
HIS CONTINUING INFLUENCE AND CONTEMPORARY RELEVANCE

David B. Suits and Timothy J. Madigan

Lucretius (ca. 99BC – ca. 55BC) is the author of *De Rerum Natura*, a work which tries to explain and expound the doctrines of the Greek philosopher Epicurus (341BC – 270BC). The Epicurean view of the world is that it is composed entirely of combinations of an infinity of sub-visible, indivisible particles—atoms—moving about in infinite space and infinite time. *DRN* was a philosophical poem, unique in part because Lucretius was trying to present in Latin verse for a Roman audience what had been presented centuries earlier by Epicurus in technical Greek prose.

The implications of the Epicurean/Lucretian view are profound: The proper study of the world is the province of natural philosophy (science); there are no supernatural gods who created the world or who direct its course or who can reward or punish us; death is simply annihilation, and so there is no next life and no torment in an underworld. Epicurus, and then his disciple Lucretius, advocated a life free from the traditional fears of death and the mysterious workings of divinities. True happiness is freedom from mental turmoil and anguish; true happiness is serenity, or, to use Epicurus's Greek term, *ataraxia*.

This collection of essays begins with William B. Jensen's "Newton and Lucretius: Some Overlooked Parallels", which investigates some influences Lucretius had on a particularly famous 17th century figure, Isaac Newton. According to Lucretius, atoms and void produce properties of matter—hardness, for example, or strength of interaction, or the experimental determination of density of matter; and likewise light was thought to be composed of very small, very rapidly moving particles. Jensen draws these and other ideas out of *DRN* and then gives them a partly symbolic form in order to show their parallels with Newton's versions.

Jensen takes to task a current view of Newton as a secret alchemist, a dabbler in magic and mysticism. "Comparison of Newton's published scientific writings with those of Lucretius and various 17th-century proponents of Epicurean atomism […] promises to provide a far more plausible explanation of the origins of many of Newton's ideas on matter, light, and even gravitation, than does the study of the alchemical literature."

The Lucretian view of the world is that it is nothing but combinations of material substance. But according to John R. A. Mayer in his essay "Lucretius— His Ideas in the Language of Our Time", such a view may be misguided. Mayer recognizes that Lucretius's purpose was to "educate his readers, liberating them from anxieties and fears", and Mayer comes to the conclusion that "intellectually I feel I am his brother, but not his twin brother". They are kin, he says, because they both reject the dominant religion of their time, because they share the belief that there is no immortal soul, and because they both hold the view that, as Mayer puts it, "there are no gods […] of the sort that people assert and praise, worship and fear".

But there are differences, too. Unlike Lucretius, Mayer is not an atomist, but rather a process philosopher who has been persuaded by the Buddhist idea of *anatta* or no-self, or, more inclusively, no substance. "I resist the notion of substance", Mayer says, "not only spirit or mind substance, but matter substance as well."

According to Charles M. Natoli ("Reflections on Paradox and *Religio* in the Evangel of Lucretius"), for Lucretius, "traditional religion's piety of temples and ceremonials is neither wanted nor even noticed by the gods and so is really no piety at all". Natoli argues that "what Lucretius scathes is nothing less than religion as his world knows it".

Lucretius's word *religio*, Natoli cautions, is not to be understood as "superstition". *Religio* is not used that way, Natoli explains, and besides,

> [T]he English term "superstition" is unfailingly unfavorable. Who isn't against it? To translate or even to understand Lucretius as denouncing "superstition" puts him in the ridiculous position of flogging a dead horse. Worse yet, it mitigates and sanitizes his provocative paradoxicality by having him flog a horse that everyone wishes were dead. But this is exactly the opposite of what he is in fact doing with his critique of *religio*.

Why does Lucretius deal in paradox? Because his message was, to Roman common sense, so very odd (and because there was a cultural distrust of the new). The message was that death was not bad, immortality was not to be desired, and the good life is not a life of power and honors, but rather an ideal of simplicity.

Lucretius thought that if the atoms—the fundamental constituents of the world—moved (or "fell") in perfectly straight and parallel lines and at the same speed, then there could be no changes—no combinations and recombinations, and hence no world. But clearly there are changes. Consequently atoms must "swerve"—thus the *clinamen*, which is an atom's spontaneous change from its otherwise vertical motion.

The title of Melissa M. Shew's essay (" 'As Stupid as the Clinamen'? Existential Aspects of Lucretius's Swerve") comes from Simone de Beauvoir's claim that although we did not choose to come into the world, it is up to us what to do with our lives: we can accept our freedom or we can insist that our lives be "as stupid as the clinamen". By means of discussions of accounts of chance in Lucretius and Spinoza, Shew presents aspects of the relationship among responsibility, error, and our place in the cosmos. "How does the affirmation or denial of chance as a metaphysical or existential principle determine how we think of human responsibility and error, particularly regarding how we can err in interpreting the nature of the universe?"

Shew points out that Lucretius affirms chance in two ways: Chance as the clinamen is a cosmological principle of creation. But chance also concerns the creative activity of our interpretation of the universe: "chance as operative *in our very investigation* of nature". For Spinoza, on the other hand, chance and fortune are superstitions; what appears to be chance is only our own failure to understand. "Against the idea of doubt, wonder, and error as mere privations [of knowledge] in Spinoza, Lucretius urges us *to* doubt and wonder so that we might see for ourselves the truth *in our very doubting*, which reveals the ways in which the clinamen is operative even in our lives." Shew argues that "we ought to prefer Lucretius's thinking about chance to Spinoza's, at least insofar as existential principles are concerned", and she brings in the work of Derrida and Bataille, for whom chance is an existential reality which must be taken into account.

She ends with:

> If we are to create or discover anything, then, according to Lucretius and Derrida, we must risk stability, take our chances, and realize, as Derrida does, that there is only "verticality and the unforeseeable" [...] — i.e., the so-called "stupidity" of the clinamen.

The issue of accident (chance, spontaneity) reappears in Vincent Bissonette's essay, " 'Half buried ... / Or fancy-bourne': Unearthed Desires and the Failure of Transcendence in Tennyson's 'Lucretius' ". The Epicurean ideal is a life of *ataraxia*—tranquility. But Bissonette shows how Tennyson sees Lucretius's goal as impossible; instead, it is an erotic obsession and a sublimated desire which becomes life-denying.

Why is tranquility not possible? Because it is disrupted by events not under the person's control. Tennyson makes use of St. Jerome's story that Lucretius's wife gave him a love potion which unexpectedly drove him to suicide. Bissonette argues that Tennyson's poem "radically questions the ideal of a human life that escapes the vagaries of chance or accident, which is exactly what the godlike state of Epicurean tranquility seems to promise. Tennyson uses Jerome's story, above all, to insist on Lucretius's human vulnerability to the actions of others, to unforeseen consequences, to unruly human passions, and to madness".

Finally, Tennyson's poem "suggests that philosophy, in hewing to a rational and scientific view of the universe, represses or *buries* the passions (especially erotic passions) that are unearthed in poetry".

But what are the boundaries of rationality? Might the rationalism of science conflict with what we usually call the humanities? Not according to Lucretius, says John R. Lenz in his essay "How Epicurean Science Saves Humanity in Lucretius". But there does seem to be a tendency to separate the two. "What is lost? Science becomes technology, the human mind does not see all it can, and uncritical religious attitudes persist." Lenz defends the benefit of Lucretius's view as a possible antidote.

Consider Aquinas: reason has to do with things of this world; salvation, on the other hand, requires revelation and faith. But for Lucretius, reason is our only salvation. Consider also the alleged fact/value distinction. Lenz reminds us that Lucretius is admired as being both an artist and a natural philosopher: "the two are inseparable in his work, where good science entails good humanity and vice versa." Consider, finally, that some people claim that humanists must protect the soul from the practical arts of manipulating matter—think of the many warnings of the dangers of science to humanity. Lucretius is certainly not anti-science, but he does not think that more inventions and technology will bring happiness, for people will simply increase their desires, want more, and continue to be unsatisfied. Instead, Lucretius says, people need science (in the broad sense of rational knowledge accessible to all persons) to achieve their full humanity and to achieve happiness, because the study of nature can free the mind from terror brought on by false beliefs—especially fear of death and fear of the gods.

"Good science", Lenz says, "makes for better humanities", and so "Lucretius is a good humanist because he is a good scientific thinker. Reason is the greatest revelation."

A central feature of the Epicurean view is that *ataraxia* (tranquility) is attainable once certain fears and prominent anxieties have been dispelled. Among these fears is the fear of death. Both Epicurus and Lucretius claim that if we understand the world correctly, we will see that death is annihilation, and annihilation is not to be feared. Here is Epicurus's argument in his *Letter to Menoeceus*:

> Accustom thyself to believe that death is nothing to us, for good and evil imply sentience, and death is the privation of all sentience; therefore a right understanding that death is nothing to us makes the mortality of life enjoyable, not by adding to life an illimitable time, but by taking away the yearning after immortality. For life has no terrors for him who has thoroughly apprehended that there are no terrors for him in ceasing to live. Foolish, therefore, is the man who says that he fears death, not because it will pain when it comes, but because it pains in the prospect. Whatsoever causes no annoyance when it is present, causes only a groundless pain

in expectation. Death, therefore, the most awful of evils, is nothing to us, seeing that, when we are, death is not come, and, when death is come, we are not. It is nothing, then, either to the living or to the dead, for with the living it is not and the dead exist no longer.[1]

In "Lucretius and Death", Dane R. Gordon finds the Epicurean / Lucretian attitude toward death unpersuasive. Consider Epicurus's claim that "when we are, death is not come". Gordon says that, on the contrary, "psychologically and emotionally, death is part of life in powerful ways, some as simple a matter as looking out for traffic when we cross the road". Moreover, "In a naturalistic world we still may be appalled by the thought of our dissolution".

"After two thousand three hundred years Epicurus's remedy seems not to have worked", because we still have a dread of death. And Gordon cautions us that Lucretius writes about the fear of death "as if it were of one kind for all people". But it is not. Nor is everyone's understanding of death the same. "A Hindu may not know the details of the life he lived before his present life, but he knows that there was a life [...] and he can surmise from his present condition what kind of life it may have been."

Lucretius claims that as we acquaint ourselves with the physical world we will be rid of our superstitions. Gordon remains unconvinced.

There is another aspect of the Epicurean attitude toward death as annihilation. Lucretius speculates that after one's death, one's atoms might by pure chance recombine just as they had been before. Would this be a kind of rebirth or re-existence? We can expand on this idea: suppose that not the very same atoms, but duplicate atoms, were to combine in exactly the way that one's original atoms had been before death. Would this be a kind of rebirth? Or consider the possibility of the kind of rebirth or reincarnation popular in Indian thought. These suggestions make us wonder if Lucretius should be willing to say that there are some grounds for thinking that death need not be annihilation. If so, death need not be "nothing to us".

In "Lucretius on Death and Re-Existence", David B. Suits argues that Lucretius should not be lured away from his original Epicurean view. Lucretius says that even if our atoms were to recombine after death, "it would not matter to us one bit". Suits calls this "Lucretius's Key", and he uses it to examine three kinds of re-existence hypotheses: recombination, rebirth, and duplication ("cloning"). In each case Lucretius's Key leads us to reject the hypothesis, not because it is false, but because it is idle.

---

1   Diogenes Laertius, *Lives of Eminent Philosophers*, trans. R. D. Hicks (Cambridge, Mass.: Harvard University Press, Loeb Classical Library, 1931), vol. 2, 10.124–126.

The papers in this collection were originally presented over two days at a conference on Lucretius at St. John Fisher College in Rochester, New York, in March 2009. At the end of the first day, the participants met for an open discussion of the ideas and issues raised that day. It was a most enlightening, delightful and educational experience.

That evening we continued our discussions over a banquet of good food and wine provided by the Department of Philosophy at Rochester Institute of Technology.

The second day of papers concluded with a decision to collect written versions of the papers into a volume for others to experience. We sincerely hope that readers of the essays in this collection will find them stimulating and rewarding.

— David B. Suits and Timothy J. Madigan

NEWTON AND LUCRETIUS:
SOME OVERLOOKED PARALLELS

William B. Jensen

EXPOSURE

Though the manuscript of the epic poem, *On the Nature of Things*, by the Roman Epicurean, Titus Lucretius Carus (96–55 BC), was first printed in book form in 1473, and in many subsequent editions, it was not until the 17th century that it began to have a significant impact on scientific thought, leading to what the Dutch historian, Eduard Dijksterhuis, has aptly termed "the mechanization of the world picture" (Dijksterhuis, *Mechanization*).[1] Sir Isaac Newton (1642–1727) was a second-generation participant in this revival of atomism, and so could build upon the earlier atomism of such 17th-century writers as Pierre Gassendi (1592–1655), Walter Charleton (1619–1707) and, especially, that of his older British contemporary, Robert Boyle (1627–1691).[2]

Examination of the "philosophical" notebook kept by Newton while a student at Cambridge shows that he was first exposed to Epicurean atomism around 1664 through the reading of Walter Charleton's 1654 work, *Physiologia Epicuro-Gassendo-Charltoniana*, whose subtitle, *A Fabrick of Science Natural Upon the Hypothesis of Atoms Founded by Epicurus, Repaired by Petrus Gassendus, and Augmented by Walter Charleton*, is perhaps more transparent to the modern reader.[3] This notebook shows that Newton explicitly favored the atoms and void of Epicurus over the competing plenum theory of René Descartes, which rejected both a lower limit to particle divisibility and the existence of an interparticle void. Whether Newton was also directly exposed as a student to the famous poem of Lucretius is not known. However, by the 1680s, when he began seriously writing the *Opticks*, he had almost certainly read Lucretius in the original, since among the surviving books of his personal library is a 1686 Latin edition of *De Rerum Natura* (Harrison, *Library*, 183), which one Newtonian scholar has described as "showing signs of concentrated study" (i.e. numbering of lines and dog-earing) (Dobbs, *Janus*, 216). Likewise, the Scottish mathematician, David Gregory, reported a conversation with Newton in May of 1694 in which Newton stated that he could demonstrate that: "The philosophy of Epicurus and Lucretius is true and old, but was wrongly interpreted by the ancients as atheism" (Newton, *Correspondence*, 338).

---

1   Bibliographic information for all references can be found in the Select Bibliography at the end of this essay.

2   For background see Kargon, *Atomism*.

3   See McGuire and Tamny, *Certain* 6, 20, 26–36, 213–215, 284. The 1654 edition of Charleton's book is available as a 1966 photo-reproduction.

However, the above connections should not be taken as implying that Newton uncritically accepted all of the tenets of Epicurean atomism. Like Gassendi, Charleton, and Boyle before him, Newton vehemently rejected the Epicurean premise that the world was created through the fortuitous collision of eternal, self-existent atoms, opting instead for a Christianized version in which God both created and directed the atoms for his own predetermined ends.[4] Newton also came to reject the Epicurean mechanism for interparticle interactions based on mechanical entanglement of complex particle shapes, favoring instead the assumption that they were the result of short-range, centrosymmetric, interparticle forces of attraction—an assumption which further fostered the view that all atoms were in fact spherical in shape.

Nor should one expect to find any explicit references to either Epicurus or Lucretius in Newton's published writings. Though he often referenced the authors of specific experimental or observational results, he was never particularly generous when it came to citing earlier anticipations of his own particular theoretical views and, in any case, by the 1680s the assumptions of atomism were already becoming a part of the accepted *Zeitgeist* in which Newton worked. In addition, Newton's religious views made him hypersensitive to the possibility that, by explicitly mentioning Epicurus or Lucretius, he might run the risk of stigmatizing his work with the charges of atheism so frequently leveled at these two classical authors. In these respects, Newton was not unlike his older, super-religious contemporary, Robert Boyle. Thus the index to the recent, complete, 14-volume edition of *The Works of Robert Boyle* contains only 28 references to Lucretius and four to Charleton, even though the historian, Robert Kargon (*Atomism,* 1966), showed many years ago that entire passages from Boyle's book, *The History of Firmness* (1659), for example, are based on direct paraphrases of Charleton's *Physiologia* of 1654.

One tactic used by Boyle to minimize the necessity of directly referring to either Epicurus or Lucretius was to adopt the suggestion of Ralph Cudworth, on the authority of Posidonius, that the atomic theory was not the invention of atheistic Greeks but of an ancient Phoenician by the name of Moschus, and that the latter was, in fact, none other than Moses of Old Testament fame (Jones, *Epicurean,* 210–211). That Newton was well aware of the Phoenician ploy is apparent from one of his few direct references in print to ancient atomism, which occurs in Query 28 of the *Opticks* when discussing opinions on the possible existence or nonexistence of an interparticle ether:

> And for rejecting such a Medium, we have the Authority of
> those, the oldest and most celebrated Philosophers of Greece

---

4   See, for example, Newton's correspondence with Richard Bentley as reprinted in Newton, *Papers and Letters,* 271–394.

---

and Phoenicia, who made a Vacuum, and Atoms, and the Gravity of Atoms, the first Principles of their Philosophy. [*Opticks*, 369][5]

Thus, while not possible to gauge the influence of Epicurus and Lucretius on Newton via direct quotation, I do hope to show that a comparison of certain passages in Lucretius with related passages in Newton's famous work on optics does provide indirect evidence of a significant influence.

MATTER AND VOID

Let us begin our comparison with what Lucretius has to say about the relative quantities of matter and void in various materials and their bearing on the observed properties of said materials:

> Since the universe is neither wholly full nor wholly empty, it follows that matter has been set apart from void discretely; thus there exist definite bodies marking off empty space from full. These atoms can neither be disintegrated when assailed by blows from without, nor be penetrated and unwoven from within, nor yet can they fail when attacked in any other way [...]. For it is seen that whatever contains no void can neither be crushed, nor broken, nor divided into two parts by cutting; nor can it receive moisture, disruptive cold, or penetrating fire, the means by which all created things are brought to an end. The more void an object contains, the more easily it is attacked by these means and falls into utter ruin. Therefore, if the first bodies are solid and without void, as I have shown them to be, they must be eternal. [1.523–540][6]

In more modern terms, what Lucretius is postulating in this quote is that such properties as the hardness of a material, its melting point (attack by penetrating fire), and its resistance to chemical attack (attack by moisture and other fluids), are a direct function of the ratio of matter to void in the material or, in more symbolic terms:

hardness, melting point, chemical resistance $= f(\phi_m/\phi_v)$ [1]

---

5   The first edition of the *Opticks* appeared in 1704, the second in 1717, the third in 1721 and the fourth in 1730. The Dover edition used here is a reprint of the 4th London edition of 1730.

6   All quotes from *De Rerum Natura* are from the translation of R. M. Geer, though other translations would serve as well.

---

where ϕ_m and ϕ_v are the fractions of matter and void, respectively, in a unit volume of the material. Note that this ratio goes to infinity whenever the fraction of void is zero, thus making true atoms infinitely hard and infinitely resistant to both melting and chemical attack.

If we now turn to Newton's *Opticks*, we find that he fully accepts these premises, though, following both Charleton and Boyle, he prefers to talk of pores rather than void:

> Now if compound Bodies are so very hard as we find some of them to be, and yet are very porous, and consist of Parts which are only laid together; the simple Particles which are void of Pores, and were never yet divided, must be much harder. For such hard Particles being heaped up together, can scarce touch one another in more than a few Points, and therefore must be separable by much less Force than is requisite to break a solid Particle, whose Parts touch in all the Space between them, without any Pores or Interstices to weaken their Cohesion. [*Opticks*, 389–390]

In other words, as per Lucretius:

$$hardness = f(matter/pores) = f(\phi_m/\phi_v) \qquad [2]$$

HARDNESS AND STRENGTH OF INTERACTION

However, the ratio of matter to void is not the only factor that affects the properties of a material. Again, in the words of Lucretius:

> Next, the same force and the same cause would destroy all things together unless eternal matter, more or less closely interwoven, preserved them; a touch would certainly be sufficient cause for destruction, for there would be no seeds of eternal body whose interweaving only an appropriate force could dissolve. But as it is, because the bonds between the atoms differ and matter itself is eternal, a thing remains with its body uninjured until assailed by a force whose keenness is a match for its own structure. [1.239–248]

Here Lucretius is telling us that a second factor—the strength of mechanical entanglement between the various particles—also comes into play. Whereas the ratio of matter to void determines the number of contact points between the various particles, the degree of mechanical entanglement (bonds between the atoms) determines the strength of those individual contact points and thus both factors, operating together, ultimately determine the overall stability of the material in question. In short:

hardness, melting point, & chemical resistance =
f(matter/void, entanglement strength)   [3]

Once again Newton tacitly accepts this model in the *Opticks*, though he replaces the mechanism of mechanical entanglement with the operation of short-range interparticle forces of attraction:

> Now the smallest Particles of Matter may cohere by the strongest Attractions, and compose bigger Particles of weaker Virtue; and many of these may cohere and compose bigger Particles whose Virtue is still weaker, and so on for divers Successions, until the Progression end in the biggest Particles on which the Operations in Chymistry, and the Colours of natural Bodies depend, and which by cohering compose Bodies of a sensible Magnitude. [*Opticks*, 394]

or in symbolic terms:

hardness = f(matter/pores, force of attraction)   [4]

DENSITY AND VOID

Finally, in a truly remarkable passage, Lucretius tells us how to experimentally determine the ratio of matter to void in a material:

> Next, why do we see that some objects weigh more than others, although they are of no greater size? If there were as much matter in a ball of wool as in one of lead, it would indeed weigh the same, since it is a property of matter to cause all things to press downward, while on the contrary empty space is always without weight. Therefore that which is of equal size and is seen to be lighter surely gives evidence that it has more void within itself. The heavier thing, on the other hand, asserts that there is more matter within itself and less void. [1.359–367]

Essentially Lucretius is telling us that the relative fractions of matter per unit volume for two materials, *A* and *B*, are directly proportional to their relative weights per unit volume or, in modern terms, are directly proportional to the ratio of their densities:

$$(\phi_m[A]/\phi_m[B]) = (density[A]/density[B])$$ [5]

This identity is likewise implicitly accepted by Newton in the *Opticks* and is applied to the question of the relative degree of rarity or rarefaction of water versus gold:

> And hence we may understand that Bodies are much more rare and porous than is commonly believed. Water is nineteen times lighter [i.e. less dense], and by consequence nineteen times rarer than Gold; and Gold is so rare as very readily and without the least opposition to transmit the magnetick Effluvia, and easily to admit Quicksilver into its pores, and to let water pass through it [...]. From all which we may conclude, that Gold has more Pores than solid Parts, and by consequence that Water has above forty times more Pores than Parts. [*Opticks*, 267]

Since the modern value for the density of water is 1 g/mL and that of gold is 19.3 g/mL, we find, on substituting into equation 5, that:

$$(\phi_m[gold])/(\phi_m[water]) = (density\ gold)/(density\ water) = (19.3)/1 = 19.3 \qquad [6]$$

or that water is, as Newton states, about 19 times "rarer" than gold.

But we can go further. Since Newton tells us that water has "above forty times more Pores than Parts" (though he doesn't tell us how he has arrived at this result), we are able to determine both the fraction of matter per unit volume and the fraction of void per unit volume in water:

$$\phi_m[water] = 1/41 = 0.024\ or\ 2.4\%\ matter \qquad [7]$$

$$\phi_v[water] = 40/41 = 0.976\ or\ 97.6\%\ void \qquad [8]$$

When substituted into equation 6, these figures allow us to also calculate the fractions of matter and void per unit volume of gold as well:

$$(\phi_m[gold]) = (\phi_m[water])(density\ gold)/(density\ water) \qquad [9]$$

$$(\phi_m[gold]) = (0.024)(19.3/1) = 0.463\ or\ 46.3\%\ matter \qquad [10]$$

$$(\phi_v[gold]) = 1 - (\phi_m[gold]) = 0.537\ or\ 53.7\%\ void \qquad [11]$$

Hence we find that the ratio of void to matter in gold is (0.537/0.463) = 1.16 or that it contains, as per Newton, slightly more pores than parts.

In the *Opticks*, Newton's interest in the question of the relative porosity or degree of rarefaction of materials was driven not by its possible relevance to questions of hardness, ease of melting, or degree of chemical reactivity, but rather by its possible relevance to how matter interacted with light. Like Epicurus, Newton viewed light as being composed of very tiny, rapidly moving particles, and he was interested in how the porosity of a body was related to its ability to transmit, reflect, refract, and/or selectively absorb these particles of light. His speculations on this subject led to the conclusion that bodies must contain far more void or pores than commonly supposed, and in order to make this conclusion more plausible to his readers, Newton performed the following hypothetical calculation:

> How Bodies can have a sufficient quantity of Pores for producing these Effects is very difficult to conceive, but perhaps not altogether impossible [...]. Now if we conceive these Particles of Bodies to be so disposed amongst themselves, that the Intervals or empty Spaces between them may be equal in magnitude to them all; and that these Particles may be composed of other Particles much smaller, which have as much empty Space between them as equals all the Magnitudes of these smaller Particles; And that in like manner these smaller Particles are again composed of others much smaller, all which together are equal to all the Pores or empty Spaces between them; and so on perpetually till you come to solid Particles, such as have no Pores or empty Spaces within them; And if in any gross Body there be, for instance, three such degrees of Particles, the least of which is solid; this Body will have seven times more Pores than solid Parts. But if there be four such degrees of Particles, the least of which are solid, the Body will have fifteen times more Pores than solid Parts. If there be five degrees, the Body will have one and thirty times more Pores than solid Parts. If six degrees, the Body will have sixty and three times more Pores than solid Parts. And so on perpetually. And there are other ways of conceiving how Bodies can be exceedingly porous. But what is really their inward Frame is not yet known to us. [*Opticks*, 268–269]

What Newton is assuming in this quote is a particle hierarchy similar to that described in his earlier statement on interparticle attractions, and that each level of this hierarchy, with the exception of the lowest or true atomic level, is composed of 50% particles and 50% interparticle pores or void. Thus the total fraction of matter per unit volume is given by the equation:

$$\phi_m = (1/2)^n \qquad\qquad\qquad\qquad\qquad\qquad\qquad\qquad\qquad\qquad [12]$$

where n is the degree of the largest particle, and the total fraction of void per unit volume is simply the difference between this value and one:

$$\phi_v = 1 - (1/2)^n \qquad\qquad\qquad\qquad\qquad\qquad\qquad\qquad\qquad [13]$$

As may be seen in the following table, which applies these equations to the cases of $n = 0...6$, for true atoms or particles of the zeroth order ($n = 0$), they give values of 1 and 0, respectively, for the fractions of matter and void, and thus a ratio of void to matter of 0; for particles of the first order ($n = 1$), they give values of 1/2 and 1/2 and a ratio of 1; for particles of the second order ($n = 2$), they give the values of 1/4 and 3/4 and a ratio of 3, etc., just as verbally summarized by Newton in the above quotation.

n	Φ_m	Φ_v	(Φ_v/Φ_m)
0	1	0	0
1	1/2	1/2	1
2	1/4	3/4	3
3	1/8	7/8	7
4	1/16	15/16	15
5	1/32	31/32	31
6	1/64	63/64	63

AN ALCHEMICAL HIATUS

To understand why the above rather obvious and somewhat trivial comparisons between Lucretius and Newton are important, and why an historian of chemistry is talking at a symposium on Lucretius about Newton, we need to look at an event that happened in the field of Newtonian studies more than 40 years ago.

It has long been known that, beginning about 1669 and continuing until about 1696, Newton devoted a great deal of his time to the laboratory study of chemistry and alchemy. While there is *nothing remotely alchemical* about any of Newton's published scientific works, a substantial quantity of manuscript material relating to his alchemical studies has survived, though this was not examined in detail by historians until the 1970s and, in particular, by the American historian, Betty Jo Teeter Dobbs, who ultimately published two monographs on the subject in 1975 (*Foundations*) and 1991 (*Janus*). Somewhat disappointingly, it turned out that the vast majority of this alchemical manuscript material consisted of transcriptions and/or translations in Newton's own hand of known alchemical books and manuscripts by various authors, as well as glossaries, bibliographies, and summaries. Regrettably, the authorship of a few of the manuscripts could not be unambiguously established, and this soon led to disputes as to whether they were actually alchemical works written by Newton himself or merely transcriptions of previously unknown alchemical works by others—a question which has still not been resolved to everyone's satisfaction.[7]

Although this material indisputably verified the fact that Newton had a strong and abiding interest in alchemy, it failed to provide definitive answers to the important questions of *why* he was interested in alchemy in the first place (and thus whether it is correct to view him as a practicing alchemist), and whether his study of the alchemical literature had provided him with important concepts which he then incorporated into his published scientific work. This lack of unambiguous evidence, however, proved no barrier to historians drawn to the subject, who simply replaced evidence with speculation. Soon a deluge of papers and books began to appear attributing virtually every aspect of Newton's scientific thought to his study of alchemy. Having supposedly proven that Newton was an alchemist, any belief or thought appearing anywhere in the alchemical literature was automatically attributed to Newton as well.

Anyone objecting to this binge of speculation was stereotyped as an outdated, semi-senile proponent of Whig history, and essentially shouted out of court. The culmination of this trend came in 1997 with the publication of a popularized biography of Newton by the science journalist, Michael White, entitled *Isaac Newton: The Last Sorcerer*, which not only took the alchemy hypothesis to the extreme but also insinuated that Newton was drawn to "occult practices and the black arts" as well (White, *Newton*, 4). Thus the great Newton, once viewed as the apex of the scientific revolution and the father of the scientific enlightenment, was reduced instead to a Faustian, schizophrenic dabbler in alchemy, magic and mysticism.

MATTER AND VOID REINTERPRETED

Nor did the material quoted earlier from the *Opticks* on the relationships between matter, void and density escape this alchemical onslaught. In 1977 Karin Figala ("Newton as Alchemist"), in a 35-page essay review of Dobbs's first book, then once again in 1984 in a 71-page article in German ("Die Exakte"), and finally, in an appendix ("Newton's Alchemical Studies") to Rupert Hall's 1992 biography of Newton, argued that, not only were these concepts found in the alchemical literature (though she never stated exactly where), but that they also

---

7 For background on these disagreements concerning authorship and further references, see Newman, *Gehennical,* Chapter 7. While discounting Newton's authorship of many of the unidentified manuscripts, Newman, not unexpectedly (given the subject of his book) attempts to argue that Newton's ideas on matter were derived from Starkey rather than from 17th-century Epicurean atomism. In addition, readers should be aware that Newman uses the word "alchemical" to describe chemical writings that are traditionally not considered to be explicitly alchemical in nature.

---

held the key to Newton's understanding of the alchemical corpus. Nowhere did she mention that these relationships were simple mathematical elaborations of those found in Lucretius and the 17th-century literature on Epicurean atomism.

Ignoring Newton's explicit statement that his hypothetical $(1/2)^n$ model was designed merely to illustrate the plausibility of the proposition that bodies are far more porous than commonly believed, and that it was in no way to be taken as a true picture of the actual structure of bodies, whose real "inward Frame is not yet known to us", Figala did the exact opposite and assumed it to be Newton's real theory of atomic structure and the key to his theory of alchemy. Though Newton explicitly discusses only the relative rarity of water, gold, and mercury in the *Opticks*, Figala expanded these examples into the triangular diagram shown in figure 1 using density values mentioned by Newton in other contexts, as well as those reported by Newton's follower, John Freind.

In this diagram true atoms appear at the apex, and materials of greater and greater rarefaction are found as one moves from the top towards the base. The numerical values listed along the right side of the triangle indicate the fraction of void in the material in question, whereas those listed along the left side indicate the fraction of matter, both values having been calculated from the material's density and the fractions of matter and void assumed by Newton for water in the same fashion as was done earlier in the case of gold. The solid horizontals connecting these numbers indicate the ratio of void to matter or "degree of rarefaction" for the materials in question, and the broken horizontals indicate the void to matter ratios calculated using the $(1/2)^n$ model and listed in the last column of the above table. Finally, in the box on the far left are listed the experimental densities of the various materials as given by Newton (N and N') and Freind (F).

There are several problems with this diagram: (1) As already noted, Figala used the term "degree of rarefaction" for the ratio of void to matter (ϕ_v/ϕ_m), whereas Newton used it for relative density or matter fraction ($\phi_m[A]/\phi_m[B]$). (2) In her calculations, Figala claimed that Newton assumed that water contained "one part matter to sixty-five parts of void"—which approximates the 1 to 63 ratio calculated from the $(1/2)^n$ model, whereas in the *Opticks*, as we have seen, Newton claimed that it contained closer to 1 in 40 parts.[8] Use of the latter, rather than the former, value obviously shifts the positions of all of the materials in the diagram relative to the hypothetical values calculated using the $(1/2)^n$ model.

Seven variations of this triangular diagram appear in Figala's 1977 article, six in the 1984 article, and one in the 1992 summary. Nowhere is it indicated where such diagrams appear in either the published or unpublished

---

8   The 1 to 65 figure for the ratio of matter to pores in water is from a fragment
      found among Newton's unpublished manuscripts (Newton, *Unpublished*, 317).
      The editors tentatively identified this as an unused draft addition to Book III,
      Proposition VI of the *Principia*, though it is very similar in content to the section
      of the *Opticks* (267) in which Newton revises his estimate to 1 to 40.

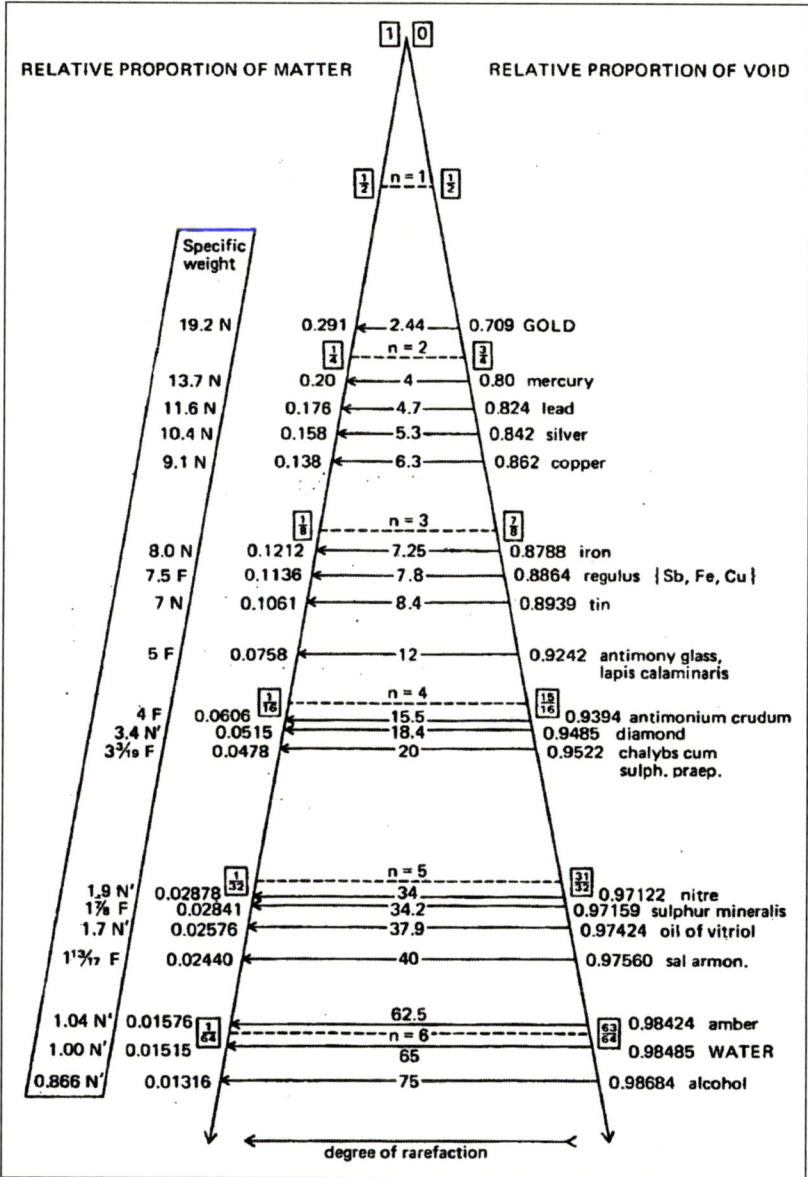

RELATIVE PROPORTION OF MATTER   RELATIVE PROPORTION OF VOID

$1,0$

$\frac{1}{2}$ — n = 1 — $\frac{1}{2}$

Specific weight

Specific weight		degree of rarefaction	
19.2 N	0.291 ←	2.44 →	0.709 GOLD
		n = 2 $\frac{1}{4}$ $\frac{3}{4}$	
13.7 N	0.20 ←	4 →	0.80 mercury
11.6 N	0.176 ←	4.7 →	0.824 lead
10.4 N	0.158 ←	5.3 →	0.842 silver
9.1 N	0.138 ←	6.3 →	0.862 copper
		n = 3 $\frac{1}{8}$ $\frac{7}{8}$	
8.0 N	0.1212 ←	7.25 →	0.8788 iron
7.5 F	0.1136 ←	7.8 →	0.8864 regulus {Sb, Fe, Cu}
7 N	0.1061 ←	8.4 →	0.8939 tin
5 F	0.0758 ←	12 →	0.9242 antimony glass, lapis calaminaris
		n = 4 $\frac{1}{16}$ $\frac{15}{16}$	
4 F	0.0606 ←	15.5 →	0.9394 antimonium crudum
3.4 N'	0.0515 ←	18.4 →	0.9485 diamond
3⁷⁄₁₉ F	0.0478 ←	20 →	0.9522 chalybs cum sulph. praep.
		n = 5 $\frac{1}{32}$ $\frac{31}{32}$	
1.9 N'	0.02878 ←	34 →	0.97122 nitre
1⅞ F	0.02841 ←	34.2 →	0.97159 sulphur mineralis
1.7 N'	0.02576 ←	37.9 →	0.97424 oil of vitriol
1¹³⁄₁₇ F	0.02440 ←	40 →	0.97560 sal armon.
1.04 N'	0.01576 ←	62.5 n = 6 $\frac{1}{64}$ $\frac{63}{64}$	0.98424 amber
1.00 N'	0.01515 ←	65 →	0.98485 WATER
0.866 N'	0.01316 ←	75 →	0.98684 alcohol

← degree of rarefaction →

Figure 1.

writing of Newton or in the alchemical literature and, indeed, a close reading of the text reveals that these diagrams are in fact the invention of Figala herself, though the figure captions fail to make this important point explicit. As such, there would, of course, be no objection to viewing them as a clever way of summarizing Newton's elaboration of the Epicurean-Lucretian theory of matter. But to do so would be a naive mistake, since this would overlook what Figala believed to be the "real" meaning of these diagrams.

Noting that these triangular diagrams have the shape of the Greek letter lambda (λ), thus allowing one to recover "the Great Pythagorean Tetraktys", Figala proceeded to point out that the ratios of void to matter calculated using Newton's $(1/2)^n$ formula, and listed in the last column of the above table, form a recurrent series which can be mathematically generalized using the recursion formula:

$$3a_n = 2a_{n-1} + 1a_{n+1} \qquad [14]$$

from which she drew the following remarkable conclusions:

> We may detect a trinitarian interpretation: three times the middle term ($3a_n$) unites in a certain way its parent ancestor ($2a_{n-1}$) and its son successor ($1a_{n+1}$); a more 'substantial' interpretation would be that a_n mediates between 'solid' (Earth) and 'thin' (Heaven), a_{n-1} being more solid than a_n and a_{n+1} being rarified with respect to a_n. Thus a_n also mediates between 'down' and 'above' and so on. Seen in an alchemical way, the 'soul' a_n mediates between 'matter' (the full) a_{n-1} and 'void' (the empty, without matter = spirit) a_{n+1}. The mediator is part of what it joins together; its nature is hermaphrodite. In traditional alchemy Mercury plays this role and on yet another level Mercurius is Hermes, the messenger of the gods, who mediates between the gods and mankind. Thus Newton's scheme has the additional advantage of conforming to magic-alchemical religious ideas. [Figala, "Newton's Alchemical", 384]

Where exactly Newton explicitly makes all of these magical-alchemical religious connections with a matter diagram which he apparently never drew or used is never explained or supported by direct quotations—it is simply asserted. If such direct evidence existed one would have thought that Figala would have been anxious to cite it, since, to paraphrase David Hume, extraordinary claims (and these are indeed extraordinary) demand extraordinary documentation. In the end, one must conclude that the ideas presented in these papers are 99% Figala and only 1% Newton. Though they may well form an intriguing approach to the interpretation of the alchemical literature, they fail to make the case that it is Newton's approach we are looking at rather than that of Figala. Rather ironically, if this was indeed Newton's approach, then it would strongly suggest that he was attempting to scientifically rationalize the alchemical literature in terms of Epicurean matter theory modified to take into account the operation of interparticle forces of attraction and repulsion—an interpretation which is strenuously opposed by most who have speculated on the nature of Newton's alchemical activities.

In the end, the effort of trying to sort speculation from fact leaves one agreeing with the evaluation given by the great British historian, Herbert Butterfield, over a half century ago, of much of the work published on the history and meaning of alchemy:

> Concerning alchemy it is more difficult to discover the actual state of things, in that historians who specialize in this field seem sometimes to be under the wrath of God themselves; for, like those who write on the Bacon-Shakespeare controversy or on Spanish politics, they seem to become tinctured with the kind of lunacy they set out to describe. [Butterfield, *Origins*, 129]

CONCLUSIONS

I hope I have shown that a textual comparison of Newton's published scientific writings with those of Lucretius and various 17th-century proponents of Epicurean atomism—something which, to the best of my knowledge (and great surprise), has apparently never been done in detail—promises to provide a far more plausible explanation of the origins of many of Newton's ideas on matter, light, and even gravitation, than does the study of the alchemical literature and would go a long way towards offsetting some of the more embarrassing excesses of the Newtonian alchemical hiatus.[9] All of this in no way negates the evidence of Newton's abiding obsession with the alchemical literature—an obsession very much in keeping with his other personal obsessions, such as Biblical prophecy or the exact dimensions of King Solomon's temple. That a great scientist may harbor irrational views on topics unrelated to his field of scientific competency is hardly a novel discovery. One could list dozens of famous late 19th-century and early 20th-century scientists who believed in psychic phenomena and spiritualism, and the present author had a roommate in graduate school, who, though now a top-ranking chemist at the National Bureau of Standards, spent much of his time as a student trying to prove the truth of astrology. Few scientists maintain a self-consistent, rational, scientific world view which extends much beyond the confines of their areas of technical specialization. Rather, like most humans, they are capable of harboring mutually contradictory views side by side in their psyches without experiencing the least degree of cognitive dissonance. As long as these personal eccentricities do not spill over into their published scientific work, their prestige as scientists remains unimpaired. The fact that Newton never attempted to publish his work on alchemy strongly suggests that he consciously

---

9   Other historians have certainly discussed Newton's atomism and its relationship to Epicurus in general terms, but none, to the best of my knowledge, has conducted a detailed comparison of specific physical points based on direct quotations as was done here. For general treatments, see Kargon (*Atomism*) and H. Guerlac ("Newton").

---

or unconsciously knew where the boundaries of acceptable mathematical physics began and ended, and attempts by some historians to forge significant links between his various intellectual "hobbies"—be they alchemy or biblical prophecy—and his published scientific legacy appear to me to be ill-advised at best and misleading at worst.

SELECT BIBLIOGRAPHY

Boyle, Robert. *The Works of Robert Boyle*, 14 vols. Edited by Michael Hunter and Edward B. Davis. London: Pickering and Chatto, 1999.

Butterfield, Herbert. *The Origins of Modern Science*. Rev. ed. London: G. Bell and Sons, 1957.

Charleton, Walter. *Physiologia Epicuro-Gassendo-Charltoniana: or a Fabrick of Science Natural Upon the Hypothesis of Atoms, Founded by Epicurus, Repaired by Petrus Gassendus, Augmented by Walter Charleton*. 1654. Reprint, New York: Johnson Reprint Corporation, 1966.

Dijksterhuis, Eduard Jan. *The Mechanization of the World Picture*. Translated by C. Dikshoorn. Oxford: Clarendon Press, 1961.

Dobbs, Betty Jo Teeter. *The Foundations of Newton's Alchemy*. Cambridge: Cambridge University Press, 1975.

———. *The Janus Faces of Genius: The Role of Alchemy in Newton's Thought*. Cambridge: Cambridge University Press, 1991.

Figala, Karin. "Newton as Alchemist". *History of Science* 15 (1977): 102–137.

———. "Die exakte Alchemie von Isaac Newton". *Verhandlungen der Naturforschenden Gesellschaft in Basel* 94 (1984): 157–228.

———. "Newton's Alchemical Studies and his Idea of the Atomic Structure of Matter". Appendix A, 381–386, in *Isaac Newton: Adventurer in Thought*, by A. Rupert Hall. Oxford: Blackwell, 1992.

Guerlac, Henry. "Newton et Epicure". In *Essays and Papers in the History of Modern Science*, 82–106. Baltimore: Johns Hopkins University Press, 1977.

Harrison, John. *The Library of Isaac Newton*. Cambridge: Cambridge University Press, 1978.

Jones, Howard. *The Epicurean Tradition*. London: Routledge, 1989.

Kargon, Robert Hugh. *Atomism in England from Hariot to Newton*. Oxford: Clarendon Press, 1966.

Lucretius. *On Nature*. Translated by Russel M. Geer. Indianapolis: Bobbs-Merrill Co., 1965.

McGuire, J. E., and Martin Tamny. *Certain Philosophical Questions: Newton's Trinity Notebook*. Cambridge: Cambridge University Press, 1985.

Newman, William R. *Gehennical Fire: The Lives of George Starkey, An American Alchemist in the Scientific Revolution*. Cambridge, Mass.: Harvard University Press, 1994.

Newton, Isaac. *Opticks, or a Treatise of the Reflections, Refractions, Inflections and Colours of Light*. New York: Dover Books, 1952.

———. *Isaac Newton's Papers and Letters on Natural Philosophy and Related Papers*. Edited by Bernard I. Cohen and Robert E. Schofield. Cambridge, Mass.: Harvard University Press, 1958.

———. *The Correspondence of Isaac Newton, Vol. 3, 1688-1694*. Edited by H. W. Turnbull. Cambridge: Cambridge University Press, 1961.

———. *Unpublished Scientific Papers of Isaac Newton*. Edited by A. Rupert Hall and Marie Boas Hall. Cambridge: Cambridge University Press, 1962.

White, Michael. *Isaac Newton: The Last Sorcerer*. Reading, Mass.: Perseus Books, 1997.

LUCRETIUS
HIS IDEAS IN THE LANGUAGE OF OUR TIME

John R. A. Mayer

I wish to thank Tim Madigan not only for organizing this interesting conference, but also for asking me to be on its program. When I was asked, I told him that while I am an academic philosopher, I am not an expert on Lucretius, with whose ideas I am essentially sympathetic, but whose work I have never really studied, never taught in my 38 years of teaching philosophy. My accepting this opportunity gave rise to the occasion of reading his work carefully and critically, coming to the conclusion that intellectually I feel I am his brother, but not his twin brother. What separates us is not only language, but 2000 years of history, and that suggests that my presentation have two parts: that which unites us, and that in which we differ. For I believe, in my existential way, that I must always speak from the perspective of being me; of speaking what I believe to be correct, even if that belief has elements in it which are based on opinion rather than deductive demonstrability, and hence, may be wrong, but nonetheless, I am committed to it as of this moment in my intellectual-spiritual development.

Consequently, I shall start with the areas of agreement, and the basis of my claiming brotherhood with Titus Lucretius Carus, who lived in Rome, relatively briefly (ca. 99 BC to ca. 55 BC). Like myself, he was a philosopher, committed to critical thinking, but not making claims to great philosophical originality. His intellectual roots were Greek, mainly Epicurean. His purpose in writing his great poem, *De Rerum Natura*, was to educate his readers, liberating them from anxieties and fears caused by common beliefs which he deemed erroneous, superstitious. In this way he, too, can be deemed existential, sharing the views he is committed to, but which are not the commonly accepted ones. This is an aspect for which I deem him to be a brother, to be very much like me.

We must set Lucretius's life into the larger historical context. The first century B.C. was a momentous historical era. It was the passing of Republican Rome to the birth of Imperial Rome. The age of Augustus was the flowering of Imperial Rome, and marked significant religious changes of the time. Augustus died in 14 AD, only 69 years after Lucretius. Up to that time Roman religion was relatively homogeneous. Under Augustus, however, not only was a new religion, the worship of the emperors, introduced, but religious pluralism developed as the Empire opened itself to many peoples, many cultures, many different religions. To make myself clear, I am not suggesting that Christianity is the impending religious change—that had to wait four centuries. The change was from homogeneity to pluralism. In that period Christianity was one of the many—a relatively minor—sects, alongside the older Roman notions, and newer versions of the worship of Isis, Judaism, Zoroaster, and Mithras were but some of the many new faiths to be found in Rome.

The weakening of the old religion is no doubt indicated by Lucretius's commitment to Epicurean materialism, and was probably also enhanced by the articulate brilliance of his poetic and rational exposition of the same. But in his time the old religion was still dominant, and his brave and explicit rejection of it makes me feel that I am kin to him, since I, too, argue against the dominant religion of my time and age, in favour of a secular pluralism, which I believe is emergent, even as it was during the successive two centuries in Rome after Lucretius.

What, then, do we, Lucretius and I, share? The belief that there is no immortal soul is one. We might express this in somewhat different language, because of our temporal separation. Lucretius admitted to the being of a soul, distinguished it from mind, life-force, and reason, but insisted that all of these are material, made of atoms, and each is to be associated with the material body. None of them could have a separate, disembodied existence. In contrast, I would say that there is no soul. But that is not a disagreement; it is just a different way of saying the same thing. Lucretius's claim that the soul is material is clearly pre-Cartesian. However, Descartes, in the 17th century, formulated very explicitly the notion that the soul is not material, but a non-material substance. This formulation was not original to Descartes; it was a notion in Lucretius's time, the very notion of the immortal soul that Lucretius was familiar with, but wished to reject and demonstrate his reasons for doing so. The Cartesian formulation, however, has worked sufficiently to ensure that for us the claim of a material soul sounds like nonsense, and thus tends to make us ignore or reject Lucretius as a philosopher, even if we admire his poetry, filled with foolish ideas.

But what he means by a material soul is clearly not nonsense, as a thoughtful reading of his text demonstrates. He suggests that the soul is to be associated with the body, and is of the same material, atomic substance as the body, and cannot properly be thought of as potentially independent of it, freed from it at death, as the believers in an immortal soul thought. His argument is both rational and persuasive. He suggests that a soul or mind in the body should be thought of as analogical to the claim that when we assert that someone has a healthy body, that health is in the body, and is of the same substance as the body. If the owner of the healthy body should become ill, the health has not escaped from the body, and does not have a now-disembodied metaphysical status; no— the now-sick body is materially different from the previously healthy one; but its disease is just an aspect, a material aspect—of the body, exactly as its previous health was. Similarly, a living body can be associated with a soul; the dead body, now a corpse, is no longer characterized by having a soul, or life, or mind, as it had previously, but none of these now has an independent spiritual existence. They were previously in the body, but now are not; yet they have no continuing autonomous existence. There is no soul, mind or life, disembodied, just as there is no ghostly health lurking out there. Today, instead of asserting the materiality of the soul, we would say that a living person is a psycho-physical entity, but would not separate psyche from soma, and then wonder about their interaction as Descartes and the Cartesians did. We simply would admit the possibility of a merely physical body, a corpse, and at the same time deny that there is any non-physical autonomous soul, mind or life. The Cartesian two-substance notion is the survival of the Roman (pre-Christian) religious superstition of an immortal soul—a superstition that was preserved in Christianity, and is still the prevalent notion. I am Lucretius's intellectual brother, because I stand with him against the prevailing view.

Of course, if there is no soul, there is no afterlife following medical death, and in that case there is nothing to be feared in anticipating dying. There is no hellfire, judgment, post-mortem punishment—be it in purgatory or in eternal hellfire; death can be faced serenely, and even if it is not desired or preferred over life, it can be acknowledged, accepted and even embraced. The Romans had no condemnation of suicide, so Lucretius did not have to fight that. In our society, in contrast, there are laws against it, and laws against arranging for a welcomed and desired death. Accordingly, I, unlike Lucretius, would welcome changing our attitudes, to allow for euthanasia and encourage loving assistance to overcome a life burdened by physical pain, hopelessness and despair. Of course I recognize potential abuses, and would work hard to prevent them and, if the prevention did not work, punish abusers—not judgmentally, but preventively, protecting society from their recurrence.

Lucretius is also certain that gods did not create the world, nor do they have power to influence it. Natural laws govern the world, and even if there are gods, humans need not fear them, nor abase themselves in awe of them. Again, he does not say that there are no gods, but merely that they are not as people imagine them. In modern language I would, in contrast, but not disagreement, say that there are no gods—neither many, nor even one—of the sort that people assert and praise, worship or fear. Material gods, made of atoms, are not real. I would simply assert that most of the images and notions associated with the word "god" or "gods" are superstitious and dysfunctional.

I might go so far as to say that I am no more an atheist than Lucretius was, but what I mean by the term "God" does not resemble most of the conventional notions. I can accept a reality that is not subject to my free will, which guides or directs me toward actions promoting compassion, justice and community, often demanding sacrifices of my money, time, comforts and first inclinations, but at the same time directing who I become and am. Thus God as love is acceptable; God as inner dialogical partner, promoting, encouraging, and even shaming me is acceptable. But that is not identical with a cosmological creator, a lord of history, or a cosmic puppeteer, directing the events that occur, or a rewarder/punisher.

In this, too, I feel a kinship with Lucretius.

I go now, to speak of our difference. I am not an atomist in the Epicurean sense. He was. He thought all matter is made up of atoms, of different sizes and shapes. His mental image was the contrast between a mound of poppy-seeds, small, light and round, and a heap of rocks or pebbles. The former moves easily, is even blown apart by a mere breath; the latter is more difficult to move. Thus, tiny, smooth atoms move easily; rougher, larger ones are more sluggish. Hence, he thought, mind, life, spirit are constituted by the lightest, roundest atoms; stuff more resistant to alteration, by larger, rougher, heavier ones. He cites the contrast between water and honey, suggesting that the slower movement of the latter is due to its larger atoms. An ingenious argument, but not my position.

I resist the notion of substance, not only spirit or mind substance, but matter substance as well. The word "substance" indicates its literal meaning, "standing under" and thus is not unrelated to the word "understanding". Atoms to Lucretius were indeed invisible, but were postulated as standing under the diverse material realities, to enable us to understand them. His atoms were not the atoms of the modern physicist, or even the molecules of our chemists, or cells of our biologists. They were mental constructs, unobservable. He accepted them, because they functioned as explanatory.

I reject them, because I am persuaded by the Mahayana Buddhist insight of *anatta*, "no-self", or, more inclusively, no substance. Reality is constituted by successive temporal moments, each filled with a huge variety of distinguishable and diverse constituents. Some earlier moments are associated with some later ones. This association gives rise in thought to the creation of words and notions that give identity to related groups. So, although 70 years ago I was a boy, later, a youth, a young man, and now, a relatively old one, there is no substantial self. "John Mayer" is a name referring to all of these interdependent aspects of reality, but there is no separate metaphysical entity, John Mayer, now this, now that, and thus substantially neither; reality is a flux of relationships, giving rise to *notions* of material substance, as well as *notions* of causal chains of relationships.

This is not enriching the metaphysics or ontology of being—a flow or flux of diverse elements. Followers of Plato, as well as Epicurus, and Hindus, are committed to *being* as the fundamental metaphysical reality. In contrast, Buddhists, Taoists, Hegelians and Whiteheadians are committed to flux or process as the fundamental metaphysical reality. Thought, reason, language and under-standing shapes this flux into entities, substances, permanencies—but taking them seriously is illusion and deception. It is taking them seriously that gave rise to the errors of Lucretius's contemporaries, i.e., thinking that there are gods and immortal souls—non-material substances; but it also misled Lucretius into thinking that there are material substances. Substances are real only as notions, as mental constructs enabling "understanding" and functioning in a rich, diverse and variedly interrelated reality. Impermanence characterizes the real—and pos-tulations about it are mere notions. This is my view as a process philosopher.

REFLECTIONS ON PARADOX AND *RELIGIO* IN THE EVANGEL OF LUCRETIUS

Charles M. Natoli

How quaint the ways of paradox!
At common sense she gaily mocks.
.   .   .   .
Ha, ha, ha, ha, ha, ha, ha, ha,
A paradox, A paradox,
A most ingenious paradox!
>   —Gilbert and Sullivan, *The Pirates of Penzance*

Sed nescio quo modo nihil tam absurde dici potest quod
non dicatur ab aliquo philosophorum. [Why I know not, but
nothing so absurd can be said but that some philosopher
may not affirm it.]
>   —Cicero, *De Divinatione*

Be it ever so well-worn, the above tag from Cicero proclaims a joyful tiding—joyful at least to the semi-mythic "every schoolboy" who, under its aegis, can shun the hard intellectual work of Philosophy not only with a clear conscience but with a smile.

But though the tag is trite, and indeed is such a commonplace that its denial could fairly qualify as paradoxical, even so—perhaps on the principle that "naked is the best disguise"—it can be taken as a pointer to a notable feature of Lucretius's poetic and philosophic endeavor, a feature whose very transparency can enable it to pass unremarked even if not quite unseen. And that is paradox.

In our day, the term is often used loosely of self-undermining or even contradictory assertions or notions, e.g., Rousseau's "forced to be free", or, in a serio-jocular vein—*ridendo dicere severum!* – "political integrity".

In a narrower, more specialized sense, philosophers and mathematicians often use it as a synonym of "antinomy", and so mean a formal contradiction deduced from assumptions whose truth is self-evident. (Or perhaps, if one may flirt with paradox in the sense next to follow—especially if the community of reference should be Cartesians—one might better say "from assumptions that are only *apparently* self-evident".)

But in an older and still very valuable sense, "paradox" means just what Gilbert and Sullivan take it to mean: an assertion that flies in the face of common sense—a willful flouting and contradicting of what we all "know" to be the case. Taken thus, it signals the brazen audacity of philosophers such as the Eleatics, who held motion and change to be unreal; or of Zeno, one of their number who argued that even swift-footed Achilles could never pass a tortoise who has a head start; or, as per the title of Cicero's own *Paradoxa Stoicorum*, of the Stoics, who maintained, for example, that all fools are equally foolish and that all who are wise are equally wise. Doctrines such as the latter, being "contrary to the opinion of all and objects of sheer amazement" (admirabilia contraque opinionem omnium) are thus called *paradoxa* even by the Stoics themselves (Cic. *Para. stoic.* 4).

Obviously, from the standpoint of common sense and common belief (*endoxa*), purveyors of paradox are, if sincere, unteachable dimwits who cannot see what is evident to even the least enlightened of the rest of mankind. Or, if paradoxical persons seem more contentious than candid, they will be taken as vainglorious poseurs. Eager to be believed by the vulgar to have surpassed the beliefs of the vulgar, they fractiously strive to palm off their absurdities as the summit of a hitherto unsuspected wisdom. It is a penchant for this sort of paradox (for contentions that, in the days of Hume and Gibbon, would have been stigmatized as "extravagant") that prompts common-sense retorts of the *nihil tam absurde* variety—retorts oft underscored with rolling of eyes, shrugging of shoulders and various hand gestures suggestive of *non compos mentis*. (Perhaps, when invoked as a ground for the not infrequent epistemic *bizarreries* of academics, this should be emended to "*non campus mentis*".)

In fine, when opinion, *doxa*, is common conviction, *endoxa*—when it is Everyman's notion of how *of course* things are—then, robed in the authority of its ubiquity and glaring obviousness, it is able to laugh its gainsayers out of court. What boots it to sit in sober judgment on a brief for the patently absurd?

Or, to vary the similitude, when common sense sits in judgment it is apt to remand those besotted and fool enough to flout it to a kind of intellectual pillory. There they will lie exposed to the jeers of those truly in the know, the commonsensical multitude: "ha, ha, ha, ha, ha, ha, ha, ha, / A paradox!"

Small wonder then that of all rhetorical or didactic tasks, that of persuasion to paradox is among the most difficult. And yet, this is the very task that Lucretius, by virtue of his mission as a kind of evangelist *avant la lettre*, has set himself. And so like his fellows he must hope, as again Cicero would have it, that "nothing is so unbelievable but that an advocate can plead it into acceptance" (*Para. stoic.* 3) [nihil est tam incredibile quod non dicendo fiat probabile].

Let us consider then, first, just why it is that as a poet and a philosophical guide, but one who in essence is an evangelist, Lucretius is constrained to traffic in paradox at all. After this we may ponder how best to understand his most glaring paradox: his scathing critique of *religio*, reverence for which is practically a constitutive element of the Roman identity.

Nova, mira falsa. [New, amazing—false.]
—Bossuet

Perhaps the most evident of Lucretius's many charms lies in the deep sense of peace that the *De Rerum Natura* exudes, one stemming not only from a feeling of blessed freedom from life's storms—as for example in the famous proem to Book 2, of which more anon—but also, and even more, from a close awareness of all of nature's moods and vestures and a profoundly accepting love of the same.

M. F. Smith, in his elegant Introduction to the Loeb edition of Lucretius (xxviii),[1] cites verses of Shelley that capture this sentiment exactly:

> I love [...]
> The fresh Earth in new leaves dressed,
>   And the starry night;
> Autumn evening, and the morn
> When the golden mists are born.
>
> I love snow, and all the forms
>   Of the radiant frost;
> I love waves, and winds, and storms,
>   Everything almost
> Which is Nature's, and may be
> Untainted by man's misery.
>
> I love tranquil solitude,
>   And such society
> As is quiet, wise and good. ["Song: Rarely, rarely comest thou", v. 25–39]

But though it is beguiling, Lucretius's Epicurean vision of the good life is one that can be expected to find much resistance in a traditionally-minded Roman public.

Like the philosopher-poet Empedocles before him, Lucretius sings the greatest theme that can be sung or reckoned upon: *rerum natura*, Nature Entire, The All. And, fittingly enough, to do so he uses all the resources at his command, whether they be the philosopher's logic (of which he has no mean grasp) or the poet's measures and similitudes. Yet he is far more than a mere philosopher-poet.

---

1   Information on references can be found in the Select Bibliography at the end of this essay.

Charles M. Natoli

Like many poets before him, and at least until Victor Hugo after him,[2] he is profoundly conscious of a bard's ability to don the mantle of a prophet and guide. But unlike the Empedocles of *On Nature*, Lucretius proclaims not just a doctrine but a gospel.[3] And unlike Hugo, Lucretius expounds a gospel that is neither of his own devising nor centered in the public sphere. Whereas Hugo proclaims in messianic terms his own opposition to Napoleon III,[4] Lucretius, heralding the therapeutic and salvific message of the divine sage-savior Epicurus, aims far higher. For he would rally his compatriots, not to good government, but to the good life.

Lucretius knows that his task will not be easy. Though he brings a message whose discoverer could only be more than man, in effect a god (cf. 5.8, 5.51), he feels he must call repeatedly for his audience's attention (2.66, 3.135, 4.931, 6.920). Moreover, he is keenly conscious of the great difficulty of gaining assent to innovations (res nova miraque menti, 5.97ff). But nonetheless he will speak out (sed tamen effabor). Beyond this, his dedication of his poem to (Gaius) Memmius, a well-known politician notable for laziness in thought and deed, corruption, sexual license, and even hostility to Epicurus, shows that Lucretius, like the Christian evangelists to come, realizes that a message of salvation is perforce addressed to the unsaved and perhaps unsavable.

In Lucretius's verse, Plato's notion of a war between Philosophy and Poetry, between the true and what is merely beautiful, between logically-tempered inspiration and inspiration unbridled, effectively finds a rebuttal. For he is a poet whose graces and charms aim not only to reveal but to demonstrate via *ratio* a truth through which alone the good life may be secured. He is thus a kind of philosophical missionary, bringing the saving "good news" of Epicurus to a public lacking the wisdom to find shelter from life's storms.

But though he is fired with enthusiasm for his doctrine—the norm,

---

2   See for example "Les Mages" in Hugo's *Les Contemplations* for his vision of the poet as being, like a priest or prophet, an anointed bearer of knowledge rooted in the divine to the common run of mankind.

> Pourquoi donc faites-vous des prêtres
> quand vous en avez parmi vous?
>
> .   .   .   .
>
> Dieu de ses mains sacre des hommes
> Dans les ténèbres des berceaux;
>
> .   .   .   .
>
> Ces hommes, ce sont les poëtes
> ("Les Mages", 1–2, 6–7, 11)

3   Empedocles's own message of salvation is the theme of his other poem, *Purifications*.

4   His "chastisements" of Louis Napoleon are of course the constant theme of *Les Châtiments*, a work brimming with his "clémence implacable".

---

really, amongst bringers of good news—he is serene in his vision of the peace of mind (*ataraxia*), the ultimate Epicurean pleasure and hence good, that he would fain impart to the unsaved.

Indeed just as, according to St. Paul, all turns to good for the elect (Rom. 8.28), so for Lucretius the pleasure of the enlightened is stoked even by the woes of those in the dark without. And so in the famous proem to Book 2 he memorably likens the man enlightened by Epicurus to one who, secure ashore during a raging storm, finds a sweet pleasure (*suave*) in watching the desperate struggles of others in peril upon the sea.

It is a scene that has often been echoed, sometimes with a nasty twist. Tertullian in *De Spectaculis* (30) famously—or perhaps, in line with the censures of Gibbon and Nietzsche, infamously—imagines himself gazing from the heights of heaven into the fiery billows of hell, all the while consumed himself by exultant laughter as he watches erstwhile enemies of the Christian faith liquefying in the flames. In like manner, Charles Maturin's main character in *Melmoth the Wanderer* laughs and gloats fiendishly as, safe on shore, he watches unfortunates whose ship has foundered struggle vainly in the waves and perish.

There might have seemed to be an acrid Melmothic whiff in Lucretius if he had not hastened to dispel it. For after affirming that the struggles of those in peril upon the deep give bliss to the watcher secure ashore, he quickly adds, not that there is joy in another's woe, but that it is bliss to look upon troubles from which one's own self is free.[5]

Needless to say, Lucretius would have his Roman audience saved onto the headland of Epicurean tranquility. But again, this is no mean task. For as Lucretius was well aware, a bringer of good news is *ipso facto* an innovator and so must to some extent be a propounder of paradox. Good news that saves is not only new but radically so. If it were a natural part or outgrowth of common belief, no evangelist would be needed to say "You are not on the way to the good life; hearken, quit your old ways and follow me!" An evangel or missionary message is thus one that will reproach or even insult an audience on the wrong track. "O wretched minds of men, O blind understandings!" (*DRN* 2.14) [o miseras hominum mentes, o pectora caeca!] But Lucretius's task will be, in some respects, even

---

5   This point finds an analogue (it can hardly be supposed to be an echo) in what is in effect Aquinas's rejoinder to the Tertullianic view. It will be given to the blessed in the kingdom of heaven, he tells us, to see perfectly the sufferings of the damned in order that their bliss may be made more delightful to them, and so that they may give more copious thanks to God. We are not told that, as per Tertullian, they will delight in the sufferings of the damned *as such*. (And yet, why not, since these torments, as the character Dante came to understand in the *Inferno*, represent the triumph of perfect justice?) But rather, as in Lucretius, the contrast with the agonies of the unsaved will heighten the blesseds' awareness of their own felicity. See *Summa Theologiae*, Supplementum, Q. 94 Art. 1.

---

more difficult than that of the Christian evangelists who succeeded him.

The Greek-speaking East primarily addressed by St. Paul and the other New Testament writers was by and large well receptive to innovation. Indeed, enthusiasm for novelty was part of its heavily Attic cultural heritage.

That Periclean Athens had a passion for novelty is the merest commonplace. Thucydides bears frequent and not uncritical witness to it, as in his Corinthians' pointed allusion to the Athenians' zeal for innovation during the congress at Sparta (1.70), and in the reproaches Kleon addresses to the Athenian assembly during the Mytilenean debate. "You are excellent men—at least for being deceived by the novelties of rhetoric [...]. You bow down like slaves before anything unusual" (3.38). We find this notion still in force, but now broadened from Athens to embrace Greece as a whole, about fifty years after Paul's death, in Tacitus's patronizing reference to the Greek mind as eager to embrace the new and startling (*Ann.* 5[6].10) [promptis graecorum animis ad nova et mira].

But Lucretius's Western, Latin-speaking Roman audience had as part of *its* cultural inheritance a deep-rooted distrust of the new. It is well-signaled by highly pejorative expressions such as *res novae*, lit. "new things", but figuratively carrying the sense of "revolution" with its attendant conflagrations and civil slaughters. In its train one can expect another outrage, *novae tabulae*, lit. "new tablets", a rhetorical shorthand for the abolition of rascally profligates' debts by wiping the accounting slates clean. On the other side are highly honorific expressions such as the rhetorically unanswerable *mos maiorum*, lit. "custom of the ancestors", which signals the "good old Roman way" from which we of the present, who are by no means up to the ancestors' mark, have alas strayed.

As Horace famously puts it,

> damnosa quid non imminuit dies?
> aetas parentum peior avis tulit
> nos nequiores, mox daturos
> progeniem vitiosorem.

> What does ruinous time not diminish?
> Our fathers' age, worse than our grandfathers',
> Gave birth to us, who will soon spawn
> Offspring yet more given to vice. [*Odes* 3.6, 45–48]

Thanks largely to the Church, in the West there derives from Rome a long tradition of hostility to the new as such, especially in the domains of politics and theology, a tradition whose power begins to wane significantly only with the Enlightenment. But that is another story.[6]

---

6   For a discussion of this theme see the author's "Révélation/Révolution: une

The novelty of his message, however, is far from our poet's only hurdle.

What is arguably the key element of Lucretius's "good news"—a death that bestows the peace of oblivion—is the very contrary of what proved to be a most attractive lure in the soon-to-triumph Christian evangel (and this notwithstanding the accompanying doctrine of hell). For Paul (1 Cor. 15.51ff) speaks in accord with what we may fairly take to be a deep human longing when he preaches as a novel doctrine ("Behold, I am telling you a mystery") the promise of eternal life. To the extent that the Elder Pliny was right in saying that to man alone of the animals is given a measureless lust for living (*Hist. Nat.* 7.1.15) [immensa vivendi cupido], Lucretius, unlike Paul, has a formidable task.

It is not an impossible one by any means. For needless to say, his Roman public does not regard death, come after what may, as an unmitigated evil. It can even be a good, as when one dies for one's country—"*dulce et decorum*", as every schoolboy used to be told, at least until Wilfrid Owen and the Somme.

Or one can simply have had sufficient of life, as Horace quietly affirms: "You have disported enough, eaten enough, and drunk enough—it is time for you to depart" (*Epist.* 2.2.214–215). [Lusisti satis, edisti satis atque bibisti, tempus abire tibi est.] Indeed, Lucretius uses the same image—"Why not, like a banqueter fed full of life, withdraw with contentment and rest in peace, you fool?" (3.938–939). [cur non ut plenus vitae conviva recedis aequo animoque capis securam, stulte, quietem?]

And it is hardly news, good or otherwise, that for Lucretius's audience suicide can be highly honorable. Perhaps the most celebrated case is that of the younger Cato, an inspiration to souls as diverse as Dante and George Washington. Declining to outlive the freedom of his country, he resolves to die—a course that is in part a practical illustration of his deep belief in one of the stoic paradoxes, viz., that only the good man is free (cf. his *Life* in Plutarch, 47).

When the elder Pliny imputes measureless lust for life to mankind, he does so in the context of a long list of evils that humans alone suffer. But Lucretius must convince his audience, not that *mere* death *can be* a good by putting paid to life at a fitting point—this would be preaching to the choir—but that a death of eternal oblivion, the dreamless sleep of an Endymion, *is* good news since it would relieve us of fear of the afterlife (another item in Pliny's catalogue of specifically human ills). And since freedom from this fear might not suffice to reconcile us to eternal extinction, Lucretius will have to go even further and argue that immortality is undesirable anyway! Just think of the colossal boredom deathlessness would bring—it would be an eternity of sameness (3.944ff).

But although eternal oblivion would indeed forestall boredom, it is equivalent to eternal inaction. And this suggests another aspect of the "hard sell"

---

réflexion sur la nouveauté dans les *Provinciales* de Pascal". An English version, slightly revised and expanded, appears in his *Fire in the Dark: Essays on Pascal's Pensées and Provinciales.*

Charles M. Natoli

Lucretius has, this time one related to life in the here and now.

The upper class Roman ideal of the good life is of a public life, one that is effectively a race (*cursus honorum*) or contest for offices and military commands, influence and prestige, wealth and power. It is a vision of the good life that to be realized requires that one be, as Longfellow put it, "up and doing with a heart for any fate".

But Lucretius's mission will compel him to convince his audience that it is much mistaken on this score, that in fact the good life lies, as Gray (who was familiar with Epicurus) would notably put it, in a sequestered, private life "Far from the madding crowd's ignoble strife". Having "lived unknown" (another Epicurean precept), and in virtuous rural tranquility ("Their sober wishes never learn'd to stray; / Along the cool sequester'd vale of life / They kept the noiseless tenour of their way"), the villagers of Gray's *Elegy* now lie unknown in the obscurity of a country churchyard. But is this an ideal that can tempt those who contend in the *cursus honorum*? Or even those of lower status who, though perhaps unable to contend themselves, nonetheless bestow their accolades on the successful?

If the simplicity of the Epicurean ideal is likely to prove a hard sell to Romans, its obscurity and inaction can be expected to be even more of an obstacle.

Many in Lucretius's audience may give a conceptual nod of approval to the ideal of frugal-living "rude forefathers". To a Roman the value of this ideal is, after all, a literary and folkloric commonplace, and moreover one that benefits from the reverence due to the *mores maiorum*. Consider for example the traditional story of Manius Curius Dentatus, a victorious consul who refused the bribes of the Samnites whilst seated at his simple hearth, roasting turnips for supper. But Dentatus, who had run through the gamut of Roman offices and honors, did not live obscurely or shun strife. To gain assent to the value of his ideal of retired disengagement Lucretius must hope that his audience, exhausted by decades of vicious civil broils spawned by attempts to win the race for honors at all costs, will now be receptive to revising its valuing. He must hope that his Romans will crave, and that the Mars he feigns to petition will finally grant, some respite (1.40) [placidam pacem], and that Memmius and other readers will come to see the "blind craving for honors" (3.59) [honorum caeca cupido] for what it truly is: a game not worth the candle, and a bar to the care-free, happy life.

In fine, then, if Lucretius is to persuade cultivated Romans of the Epicurean ideal, if he is to "make straight the way" of his master Epicurus, then his road will be beset with paradoxes that his audience is likely to find (if one may be permitted another biblical image) just so many "stones of stumbling". And nothing noted so far is likely to be so great a stone of stumbling to a Roman audience as Lucretius's deliberately provocative and paradoxical treatment of religion, *religio*.

The church bells toll a melancholy round,
> Calling the people to some other prayers,
> Some other gloominess, more dreadful cares,
More hearkening to the sermon's horrid sound.
Surely the mind of man is closely bound
> In some black spell [...].
> —Keats, "Written in Disgust of Vulgar Superstition"

When I mention religion, I mean the Christian religion; and not only the Christian religion, but the Protestant religion; and not only the Protestant religion, but the Church of England. [...] [To say that this] will uphold, much less dictate, an untruth, is to assert an absurdity too shocking to be conceived.
> —Reverend Thwackum in Fielding, *Tom Jones*

If one wished to explain to a wide audience what, in a Roman's eyes, were the crucial qualities that made up and distinguished from others a true Roman, one could hardly do better than to examine the character of Vergil's Aeneas. His piety towards gods, kin and fatherland combined with his stick-to-it-iveness and high seriousness in the face of incessant obstacles make him at once the prototype and the ideal Roman.

Pious Aeneas is so much a man of *religio* that he follows the gods' plans and promptings even after his goddess mother, having lifted the veil that clogs his mortal sight, shows him the pitilessness of the great gods as they destroy Troy from its foundations. The city falls, she blandly explains, not on account of the guilt of Paris and Helen but owing to the gods' merciless ferocity—"divum inclementia, divum" (*Aen* 2.602). The repetition is like a hammer blow. But Aeneas almost immediately obeys Jupiter-sent omens nonetheless. His is a piety so puzzling on its face—why on earth would one reverence and follow gods like *these*, gods against whose blows piety is of no avail?—that at least one great modern commentator has found the message of the *Aeneid* to be simply irrational at this point.[7] But with or without reason, Aeneas's piety towards the gods remains intact and he will remain faithful to the mission Jupiter has ordained for him. In following Epicurus by vehemently assailing what prevails as *religio*, Lucretius is attacking, not just a set of entrenched beliefs and practices, but a highly valued and even foundational element of the Roman self-image.

---

7   See p. xxi of R. G. Austin's humane Introduction to *P. Vergili Maronis Aeneidos Liber Secundus*.

His target is also a linchpin of the Roman state, inextricably entwined as it is with ceremonials designed to honor, to propitiate, to petition, and above all to cooperate in partnership with the gods on a quid pro quo basis.

Like all evangelists, Lucretius would have his audience quit the old way for the new—in this case, to abandon *religio* in the quest for the happy life rather than vainly seeking to secure the happy life through *religio*. But this is in effect to exhort his Roman audience to be decidedly less Roman. At this level his mission is as provocative as it could well be, a summons to *res novae* in public life, private practices and self identification.

That Lucretius is well aware of the paradoxical character of his message is clear. Having trumpeted the triumph of Epicurus in freeing human life, hitherto crushed to earth by the weight of religion (1.63) [in terris oppressa gravi sub religione], the poet is not surprisingly afraid that his Roman audience may balk at joining him in trampling *religio* underfoot. Perhaps, he deadpans, you will find these elements, these first footsteps in Philosophy, to be impious and a path to wrongdoing (1.80–82). And so indeed prevailing *doxa* would have it. But Lucretius immediately and boldly counters with paradox.

> quod contra saepius illa
> religio peperit scelerosa atque impia facta.

> Rather, on the contrary it is more often
> That religion of yours which has given birth to criminal and
> impious deeds. [1.82–83]

That is, *religio*, the very paradigm of piety, is—as in the example that follows (Agamemnon's sacrifice of his daughter Iphigenia)—a mighty source of impiety, of unholy wickedness![8] Like Catullus's "impious religion of the Persians" (90.4) [Persarum impia religio], Lucretius's formulation is as arresting as it is oxymoronic.[9]

Now Catullus, even if only for poetical and rhetorical purposes, concedes that the nasty Persian religion might be true (si verast), foreign gods being what they are, one supposes. But if Lucretius's paradoxical comment is true, then what must he hold piety truly to be? And what must true *religio* be?

---

8   Cf. his famous "So great has been the power of religion in persuading to evil" (1.101) [tantum religio potuit suadere malorum], a line that Voltaire (speaking here as Memmius) prophesied would last as long as the world (*Lettres de Memmius à Cicéron*, 2).

9   Cf. "This assertion, in the structure of traditional Latin, is madness. On the basis of the meaning of Latin words, it cannot be true" (John Douglas Minyard, *Lucretius and the Late Roman Republic*, 37).

It is striking that neither *religio* nor its cognates occur in a favorable sense in Lucretius. Yet one could fairly say that in his thought, just as the traditional religion is impious, so in a manner of speaking the true religion would be profane and the true piety superstitious. But as none of these rather Chestertonian formulations can be well weighed without a prior understanding of his doctrine of the gods, and since this in turn rests on his understanding of what is real, a very summary account of the latter might not be out of order. The reader whose tastes, like those of Memmius in Voltaire, do not run to natural philosophy can overleap it with relative impunity.[10]

*

The two most fundamental kinds of thing are *corpus* (matter, body) and *inane* (void). Body's existence is proved by the senses; the fact of motion implies the existence (so to speak) of void. (If *inane* were not a real thing, motion could not be real. But paradoxically this "thing" *inane* is in effect a nothing, for as its name implies it is but an empty nothingness into which bodies can move.)

The crucial point that there can be no third ultimate category (*tertia natura*), and therefore that only matter and empty nothing can exist, follows from their definitions as not merely contraries but contradictories (1.430ff). Matter is taken as equivalent to what is tangible, even should its touch be imperceptible to us; void is equivalent to what is non-tangible (*intactile*).[11]

All body is composed of minute, imperceptible elements whose Greek name (*atomoi*, "uncuttables") rightly implies that they cannot be subdivided.[12]

---

10 Immediately following the hyper-laudatory prophecy referenced in n. 8 above ("Ce beau vers . . . durera autant que le monde") comes Memmius's "S'il n'était pas un physicien aussi ridicule que tous les autres, il serait un homme divin".

11 If for Lucretius void should be properly understood as a non-existence, then he would be a materialist (only matter is real) who effectively begs the question of materialism's truth. For the assertion of equivalence between the categories of void and the intangible implies, not only that all that is void (empty nothingness) is intangible, which is obviously true, but also the very debatable claim that all that is intangible is empty nothingness (and hence non-existent).

To make the latter claim is to assume that whatever *is* existent must be tangible (matter), i.e., that materialism is true. But even if it were bound up in no circularity of reasoning, the claim that all that is intangible is non-existent is one that has divided philosophers for millennia, and so is far too problematic for its truth to be merely assumed as Lucretius does here.

12 If matter *were* capable of infinite subdivision, then atoms, like all other material things, would be composed of an infinite number of parts. But as each of a thing's infinite number of parts would have some magnitude, every material object (atoms included) would occupy an infinite amount of space. As this is clearly false,

---

Since all atoms rest on void, they must all be falling downward (2.217).[13] Moreover, they must all be falling at the same rate, heavy and light alike, since void offers the same resistance—none!—to the fall of each atom (2.225ff). But this means that collisions between atoms, which are necessary if they are to form aggregates (*concilia*), must be caused by a sideways motion, the famous *clinamen* or swerve (2.216ff). Since the natural downward motion of the atoms cannot cause it, the swerve must be spontaneous and uncaused, a factor which also allows the will to be free of absolute causal constraint (2.251ff).

Irrational though a spontaneous, uncaused phenomenon may appear to be—and though it is at odds with his earlier argument, meant to dispel belief in effectively miraculous intervention in nature by the gods, that nothing can come out of nothing (1.146ff)—Lucretius cannot but infer the swerve.

For he must choose between the *clinamen* and the rest of Epicurus's atomic theory. Since compound material objects and free will incontestably exist, then—if Epicurus is right about the existence of atoms and their inescapable downward motion—swerve there must be. But just as the housemaid famously excused her out-of-wedlock baby on the grounds that "it was just a little one", even so Lucretius, who seems to be aware that he is heavily taxing his audience's credulity, is at pains to insist that the swerve is ever-so-small (2.243–244). At the end of the day, however, Lucretius seems to have decided that the truth of the *clinamen* would be less miraculous than the falsehood of the rest of his master's theory.

In any event, the willingness of Lucretius to espouse the *clinamen* shows that, after the manner of the modern physicist, he treats common sense notions such as the causal principle to be a theory of very wide but still limited scope. Some things are for a reason, but other things just are. For that matter, the very existence of atoms falls into the latter category. "Why is there anything rather than nothing?" is a question that Lucretius, in common with other ancient cosmologists, pointedly ignores.

Since vision is possible because bodies radiate films of atoms (*simulacra*) corresponding to their shapes (4.26ff), it follows that there must be gods, for they are sometimes perceived by the minds of mortals, especially in sleep (5.1169ff, 6.76–78). That they are seen most often in this state is owing to the very fine, tenuous nature of the atoms of which they are composed.

*

---

then, by *reductio ad absurdum*—a favorite type of argument with Lucretius—matter is not capable of infinite subdivision, and so the smallest bits of matter must be indivisible (1.615ff).

13 Properly speaking, "downward" is impossible given Lucretius's view that the universe must be infinite. It is odd, though, that he speaks this way given that he has already told us that in an infinite universe there can be no middle (1.1068ff, though the lines are incomplete).

A culture's criteria for divinity are in the highest degree revealing. How much more than human must something be in order to be accounted divine? How high is the high bar, so to speak? For example, the Norse peoples had a rather low bar: their moody and grim divinities not only had a beginning but were bound by fate to die violent deaths.

Though not as high as ours, the Romans' standards were higher. They envisioned the gods as by nature immortal. Still, they were limited in knowledge and power (Jupiter is a possible though equivocal exception) and could all display morals that were dubious or worse. But the Platonically grounded inflation in the concept of divinity that was to flower in the Christian tradition is clearly gathering strength by the time of Vergil and Lucretius. It is perhaps best signaled by the growing sense of incompatibility between divinity and evil and imperfection. Could a world so flawed as this one have been made by gods, or could the mind of a goddess harbor hatred towards even a pious man? This tradition's fruition in the notion of God as one, all-powerful, all-knowing and all-good—a notion culminating in Anselm's "that than which no greater can be conceived"—eventually succeeds in making the idea, not only of a mortal, but of a bad or limited god frankly inconceivable.

To stay in keeping with the classical tradition's conception of divinity and immortality as being so bound together as to be effectively one and the same[14]—a conception so deeply entrenched that its denial would appear incoherent—Lucretius is forced into an anomaly. He must aver that the gods' tenuous bodies form an exception to the otherwise universal rule that all things composed of atoms will eventually discompose and so perish. (This de facto dualism of matter[15]—atoms which can form permanent *concilia* vs. those which cannot—all but makes the gods' substance to be the "third nature" that Lucretius argued was impossible at 1.430ff.)

Indeed, the tenuous composition of their bodies matches that of their dwellings (5.146ff), the spaces between the worlds where they dwell in

---

14 In something like an anticipation of Anselm's ontological argument for the existence of God (briefly, that the essence of God as evidenced in his concept implies the fact of his existence), Lucretius asserts that the very nature of gods is inextricably bound up with immortality (and, more curiously, tranquility). See 1.44–45 (repeated at 2.646–648). Interestingly, at 1.440 he implies that matter too exists per se, i.e., that *corpus* itself, like the *concilia* which are divinities, also exists through its own nature and so exists necessarily. On per se existence, see also 1.419, 422, and 479. See too Smith's note on 1.422 in the Loeb edition.

15 For another seeming dualism of matter in Lucretius see 5.151, where the gods' matter is said to be untouchable by anything we can touch, even though matter (*corpus*) was earlier affirmed to be coextensive with what is tangible (1.430ff). However, given the line that precedes it, possibly the former passage means "untouchable by us" in the sense of eluding our body's (though not our mind's) awareness of its impact.

Epicurean tranquility (3.18–24). As they are blissfully indifferent to a universe that is far too imperfect for us to suppose that they created it for us (5.195ff), we have nothing to fear or to hope for from them. However they can and should serve as exemplars and inspirations to us as we strive to survey all things with tranquil mind as do they (5.1203).

Thus traditional religion's piety of temples and ceremonials is neither wanted nor even noticed by the gods and so is really no piety at all (5.1198) [nec pietas ullast]. Even worse, the crimes traditional religion has prompted and its slanderous tales of divine folly and malfeasance make it a shockingly paradoxical *religio impia*.[16]

It follows that for Lucretius true religion should be, in the term's root sense, profane. For the striving for a life worthy of the blissful Epicurean gods is very much an individual affair. And so is becoming strong enough to receive with peaceful mind the gods' *simulacra* and thus to know their divine shapes (6.76–78). Not only is there no reason for these to take place in the public arena of state-sponsored ceremonials and worship, but they will be easier in private, "outside of the fane" with its distracting crowd and vain prayers.[17]

And it is because of this private, personal aspect that we could say— oxymoronic though it seems—that for Lucretius, true piety is in one sense superstitious, *superstitiosa*. For the term and its cognates are by no means always pejorative. Its root sense suggests its original meaning, to stand still in the presence of a thing as in awe or dread. Taken in this way it implies an individual's private access to divine secrets (e.g., one's ability to divine the future) and by extension an individual's own particular religious exaltation or belief.[18]

---

16   Guido Milanese picks up on this idea nicely in his translation of Lucretius
     (*La Natura delle Cose*) when he subtitles a section consisting of lines 1.80–102
     "Empietà della religione".

17   Lucretius does tell us that the unenlightened will not visit the shrines of the gods
     [delubra deum] in a tranquil spirit [placido cum pectore] (6.75). This need not
     be taken to suggest that the Epicurean sage *will* visit them in such a spirit. And so
     although the sage, unlike the devotee of traditional religion, will be able to receive
     the divine simulacra with peace of mind [animi tranquilla pace], it does not follow
     that this will be in a shrine or temple. Per contra, Smith writes: "And although
     the wise man will not worship the gods or make sacrifices to them in the hope of
     influencing them, he will participate in religious ceremonies, for this will make
     it easier for him to concentrate his attention on the divine *simulacra*" (xxxviii). It
     is hard to see, though, why such concentration should be helped by attendance at
     public worship. If anything, Epicurean piety will be more difficult there given that
     the ceremonials for the falsely conceived gods of traditional religion will voice
     fears, seek favors, etc. Cf. 1.102ff.

18   For the term's root and original senses see Lewis and Short's dictionary, s.v.
     "*superstitio*". For the sense of religious exaltation, especially in one who feels

> And now I was sorry that God had made me a man. [...] The beasts, birds, fishes, &c., I blessed their condition, for [...] they were not to go to Hell-fire after death; I could therefore have rejoiced, had my condition been as any of theirs.
> —John Bunyan, *Grace Abounding to the Chief of Sinners*, #87–88

> religio deos colit, superstitio violat.
> [Religion honors the gods, superstition wrongs them.]
> —Seneca, *De Clementia*

Though Marx famously considered religion to be the opium of the masses, no one translating him would dream of rendering the German term "Religion" by "opium of the masses". For inasmuch as his understanding of "Religion" is theory-laden, it is up to his theory to prove it. In that event, the fair reader could be expected to come to the same understanding of religion as Marx. But to anticipate the reader's conclusion is not the job of the translator.

For like reasons, where our term "superstition" is the most misused and misleading in a Lucretian context is, alas, precisely where it has most often appeared, namely, as a translation[19] or gloss of "*religio*" as though "superstition" and not "religion" were the true object of his attack.[20]

The critique of *religio* to which Lucretius gives pride of place (for it directly follows the great encomium of Epicurus in book one) concerns its propensity to spawn crime and impiety (1.80–101). His account there of the sacrifice of Iphigenia has become one of the poem's most famous passages.

The story of her immolation to Artemis to secure the Greek fleet fair winds to Troy lends itself to powerful dramatic retelling, especially given the pathos (and dubious *pietas* regarding kin ties) of her father Agamemnon's participation. And though the story shows Romans that under religion's baneful spell even the Greeks, a people of high culture, could stoop to such barbarities, nonetheless the choice of this incident by Lucretius is a rather curious one.

True, it is well calculated to jar on Roman sensibilities, to which human

---

able to prophesy, see the *Oxford Latin Dictionary*, s.v. "*superstitiosus*" (1). On the individualistic overtones of *superstitio* and its cognates see Dale B. Martin, *Inventing Superstition* 126–127.

19 For example, by Bennett, Smith, Latham and more recently by Slavitt.

20 "*Superstitio*" and its cognates do not appear in Lucretius. However, the hideous aspect of *religio* is said to be "super [...] mortalibus instans" in 1.65, which Smith cites as partial reason for his rendering of "*religio*" as "superstition" (Loeb, p. 8 note a).

Charles M. Natoli

sacrifice appeared both appalling and alien.[21] Yet this sensibility could buckle under stress. When panic gripped the city after the disaster at Cannae in 216 BC the Romans, guided by the Sibylline Books, buried alive two couples, one of Greeks and one of Gauls, in the *forum boarium*. Similar sacrifices, prompted by fear of a Gallic invasion, occurred in 228 BC and 113 BC. Why did Lucretius not seize instead on one of these well-known historical incidents for censure? They were, after all, spawned directly by traditional Roman *religio*.[22] Perhaps this would have been hitting a bit too close to home as well as reminding his audience of the presumed nexus between *religio* and the welfare of the state. Or then again, perhaps these episodes simply lacked the enhanced horror that comes from Agamemnon's impious violence to what is owed from a father to a child.

But the chief philosophical focus of Lucretius's charge against *religio* emerges immediately after the story of Iphigenia. It is that religion not only prompts us to evil but is itself an evil, one that binds us in fear to proud masters. For it poisons life with terror of ills that angry or jealous gods are thought to visit on mortals in this life and the next (1.102–111). It is precisely this that Vergil seizes on as paramount in his famous praise of Lucretius in *Georgics* 2.490–492. He has, we are told, trampled all fear underfoot (metus omnis […] subiecit pedibus)—an obvious echo of Lucretius's own poem in which religion, which before Epicurus had ground *us* underfoot, is now, thanks to him, cast under ours (1.78–79) [quare religio pedibus subiecta vicissim obteritur].

Is it not therefore superstitious fear of the sort voiced so tellingly by Bunyan that is Lucretius's real target? And why then should we not translate or gloss "*religio*" as "superstition", especially given that "*superstitio*" is the Latin term commonly used to render the Greek *deisidaimonia*, lit. "fear of divinities"?

First of all, the English term "superstition" is unfailingly unfavorable. Who isn't against it? To translate or even to understand Lucretius as denouncing "superstition" puts him in the ridiculous position of flogging a dead horse. Worse

---

21 The Senate formally outlawed human sacrifice in 97 BC. The elder Pliny's account of its role in the Persian religion well reveals it as something foreign to Roman thinking (*Nat. Hist.* 30.1–2, 12–15).

22 In Mary Beard, John North and Simon Price's *Religions of Rome*, we read that on these occasions we are not dealing with "sacrifice in terms of the normal Roman ritual; so far as we know there was no immolation of the victims, no act of killing, no return of *exta* [entrails] to the gods. It was not therefore strictly inconsistent of the Romans to have forbidden human sacrifice, as they did later on; for according to the formal religious rules this killing was not a sacrifice" (vol. 1, 81). But even though they do not lie within the hedge of these qualifications the killings are indeed sacrifices. And though not a part of "normal Roman ritual" they are clearly tied to traditional *religio* by virtue of being intended to propitiate recognized divinities and by being prompted by interpretation of the Sibylline Books. (This task was in the charge of the books' Senate-appointed custodians, the *decemviri sacris faciundis*.)

---

yet, it mitigates and sanitizes his provocative paradoxicality by having him flog a horse that everyone wishes were dead. But this is exactly the opposite of what he is in fact doing with his critique of *religio*, a term that in Latin is almost unfailingly honorific.[23] And while it is true that "*superstitio*" is commonly used to render the fear-proclaiming Greek "*deisidaimonia*", the latter term, like "*superstitio*" itself, is by no means always pejorative.[24] It can even, like our expression "fear of the Lord", simply suggest religious awe and reverence and so be positive, as in "The fear of the Lord is the beginning of wisdom" (Prov. 1.7).

Secondly, "*superstitio*" to a Roman is highly suggestive of foreign, un-Roman religious belief or practice. It denotes "ideas and rituals that did not—indirectly or explicitly—have the approval of the Senate and priesthoods in the public or private sphere, and which could potentially be regulated or forbidden by order of the Senate".[25] For a near analogue we might think of the dismissive, rather contemptuous expression "fancy religions" in the old story of the Victorian drill sergeant sorting out troops for Sunday morning church parade. "Protestants to the right, Catholics to the left, and fancy religions in the middle." The closest thing to "*superstitio*" in English might be "outlandish religion". This would capture both the sense that it is alien and the accompanying attitude of supercilious rejection.

In a curious, seemingly anomalous passage in Minucius Felix we are told that the god of the Christians is so obscure that he is unknown even to

---

23 Cassell's Latin dictionary, unlike that of Lewis and Short and the *Oxford Latin Dictionary*, is misguided, I think, in giving "superstition" as a possible meaning of "religio" (1a). Two citations are given in support. One is from Lucretius himself, in whom the meaning of *religio* is treated in the present essay. It is the famous "tantum religio potuit suadere malorum" (1.101). [So great has been the power of religion in persuading to evil.]. The other is from Livy. But the *religio* that he is alleged to use in the sense of "superstition" is not mere *religio* but the term in a highly qualified sense: "multiplex religio et pleraque externa" accompanied by new rituals, "novos ritus" (4.30.9). The former expression is straightforwardly "various kinds of religious practice, mostly foreign" (Valerie Warrior in the Hackett translation) or "all kinds of religious practices, many of them foreign" (T. J. Luce in the Oxford World's Classics). A few lines later, when Livy wants to impute a superstitious mentality to those taken in by these practices—no surprise, given that he has called our attention to their foreignness and their novelty—he calls them "capti superstitione [not 'religione'] animi" (Warrior: "superstition-prone people"; Luce: "people's superstitious susceptibilities"). Even if we understand Livy to say that these religious practices are themselves superstitious, this would not imply that "religious" *meant* "superstitious" in that context. (No more than to say "Various new foreign breeds of dog are vicious" would entail that "dog" *meant* "vicious" in that context.)

24 Cf. Martin, *Inventing Superstition* 5–8, 18–20.

25 Susan Williams Rasmussen, *Public Portents*, 213. See pp. 212–217 for examples and for a helpful discussion.

Charles M. Natoli

Roman superstition: "non saltem romana superstitio" (*Oct.* 10) has heard of him. This expression can be jarring, and all the more so as is put into the mouth of a Roman follower of the traditional religion, unless we remember that it can simply designate a foreign cult recognized by the Senate. The sense here is simply that the Christian god is such a nobody that not even the usual "fancy religions" know anything of him.

But though it is ordinarily dismissive rather than merely descriptive, "*superstitio*", even when it is meant to indict, need not be so powerfully pejorative as one might think. This point is signposted by the practice of Roman authors— if indeed it is not simply that their indignation impels them to pile Pelion on Ossa—to qualify it in a negative way when they wish to denounce vigorously. Thus Christianity is not sufficiently disparaged by calling it a mere "*superstitio*". Rather, it is also empty and crazy, "vana et demens superstitio" (Min. Felix, *Oct.* 9); depraved and excessive, "superstitionem pravam et immodicam" (Pliny, *Ep.* 10.96.8); new and evil-working, "superstitio nova et malefica" (Suet. *Nero* 16); destructive, "exitiabilis superstitio" (Tac., *Ann.* 15.44); and so forth.

* * *

Though its genre permits and perhaps even requires a measure of self-indulgence, an essay should not descend into a bacchanal, and it may be that we have reveled in paradox to a point that would sate even a Chesterton. "Sat lusisti, tempus est abire." But before departing, a few summary remarks might not be amiss.

Lucretius preaches to no choirs, nor does he mean to, but rather to an audience whose likely resistance is well figured by the Memmius to whom the *De Rerum Natura* is addressed. In seeking to demolish *religio* and so to clear the ground for the Epicurean good life, of set purpose he audaciously goes beyond mere provocation and crosses over into paradox.

The *religio* he flays is precisely what his audience understands by the term—the cult of the gods as practiced and reverenced by it. But he not only has the audacity to argue that as a set of beliefs it is false, a trait he shares with skeptical compatriots who value *religio* merely as what Rousseau would later call "civil religion". He has the impudence to argue that it is impious as well. We falsify, mitigate and palliate Lucretius's uncompromising critique if we contort him into a Thwackum-esque "By religion I mean false religion. By false religion I mean superstition. By superstition I mean tales spawning complicity in crime and fear of the gods. By fear of the gods I mean neither reverence nor awe but craven terror. To think that such clarity could be a source of confusion, that it could uphold much less dictate a misunderstanding, is to assert an absurdity too shocking to be conceived." What Lucretius scathes is nothing less than religion as his world knows it.

In further opposition to Roman ideals Lucretius preaches a vision of the good life that is profoundly quiescent, passive and private. Indeed, insofar as its goals, friendship aside, consist in *refraining* from much of common life, and in a pleasure (*ataraxia*) that is an *absence*, the Epicurean good life can be seen as a sort of un-life, a negation consisting of non-doing and non-feeling and thus a "mortal life" in the qualifier's most literal sense. As such it nicely prefigures its Epicurean sequel, the likewise oxymoronic *mors inmortalis* that awaits us all "when immortal death [for it is an eternal feature of the cosmos and eternal state for us] takes away mortal life" (3.869) [mortalem vitam mors cum inmortalis ademit]. It is a far cry from the Roman conception of Philosophy as something well left for old age when the time for action has passed and the contentions of the public arena are behind one.

Finally, the prominence of paradox in Lucretius's message should occasion little surprise. For, in a final paradox, every evangelist, until and unless his good news triumphs, is perforce also a dysangelist. His message cannot be good news without shadow or alloy. Inevitably, as the old saw would have it, there's good news and there's bad news.

The evangel? He that hath ears to hear let him hear! The good news is at hand, and by it ye can be saved even as I. That the happy life may be secured by it is shown by the example of the master himself.

The dysangel? The good news is, after all, new. It follows that the old ways, the *mores maiorum*, are not so good news. In fact, they are what you need to be saved from! Quit them, then. Learn to live the truly good life—put you on the lord Epicurus—rather than be content to live merely a good Roman life, or a good Hellenic one.

But it is an ungrateful world that we live in. How unwelcome, and how hard a sell an evangel can be, both on its own account and on that of its accompanying dysangel, can be readily appreciated from the number of evangelists who, far from receiving the traditional reward (*euangelion*) for bringing the good news from Ghent to Aix, so to speak, ended up on a cross like Jesus or Mani—or, like Epicurus and Lucretius, suffered from centuries of distortions and downright slanders.

And so, alas, full many an evangelist has found that, despite his utmost zeal, obstinate mankind shows itself incredibly resistant to truth. At the end of the day, as one of them glumly reflects, the dog returns to its vomit and the pig to the mire. It is almost enough to make one think that there is some original defect in our species that blights its understanding and turns it from the good. But that view belongs, not to the message of Lucretius, but to the dysangel of another evangel, one that climbed the hard path to success by denying him.

SELECT BIBLIOGRAPHY

Austin, R. G. Introduction to *P. Vergili Maronis Aeneidos Liber Secundus*. Edited by R. G. Austin. Oxford: Oxford University Press, 1964.

Beard, Mary, John North, and Simon Price. *Religions of Rome*. Cambridge: Cambridge University Press, 1998.

Livy. *The History of Rome: Books 1-5*. Translated by Valerie M. Warrior. Indianapolis: Hackett, 2006.

———. *The Rise of Rome: Books 1-5*. Translated by T. J. Luce. Oxford: Oxford University Press, 1998.

Lucretius. *Titi Lucreti Cari De Rerum Natura Libri Sex*. Edited with Prolegomena, Critical Apparatus, Translation and Commentary by Cyril Bailey. 3 vols. Oxford: Clarendon Press, 1947.

———. *De Rerum Natura*. Edited by Martin F. Smith. Translated by W. H. D. Rouse and Martin F. Smith. Cambridge, Mass.: Harvard University Press, Loeb Classical Library, 1992.

———. *On the Nature of Things*. Translated by C. E. Bennett. Roslyn, New York: Walter J. Black, 1946.

———. *On the Nature of the Universe*. Translated by R. E. Latham. London: Penguin Books, 1951.

———. *On the Nature of the Universe*. Translated by Ronald Melville. Oxford: Oxford University Press, 1997.

———. *The Nature of Things*. Translated by A. E. Stallings. London: Penguin Group Ltd., 2007.

———. *De Rerum Natura*. Translated by David R. Slavitt. Berkeley: University of California Press, 2008.

———. *La Natura delle Cose*. Translated by Guido Milanese. Milan: Mondadori, 1992.

Martin, Dale B. *Inventing Superstition: From the Hippocratics to the Christians*. Cambridge, Mass.: Harvard University Press, 2004.

Minyard, John Douglas. *Lucretius and the Late Roman Republic*. Leiden, Holland: Brill, 1985.

Natoli, Charles. "Révélation/Révolution: La Nouveauté dans les *Provinciales* de Pascal". In *Le Savoir au XVIIe siècle*, 243–253. Edited by John D. Lyons and Cara Welch. Tübingen, Germany: Gunter Narr Verlag, 2003.

———. *Fire in the Dark: Essays on the* Pensées *and* Provinciales *of Pascal*. Rochester: University of Rochester Press, 2005.

Rasmussen, Susan Williams. *Public Portents in Republican Rome*. Rome: L'Erma di Bretschneider, 2003.

Smith, Martin Ferguson. Introduction to *De Rerum Natura*, by Lucretius, ix–lxv. Translated by W. H. D. Rouse and Martin F. Smith. Cambridge, Mass.: Harvard University Press, Loeb Classical Library, revised edition, 1992.

"AS STUPID AS THE CLINAMEN"?
EXISTENTIAL ASPECTS OF LUCRETIUS'S SWERVE

Melissa M. Shew

Yet consider how nobody now, jaded by seeing it so much,
thinks it worth gazing up into the brilliant regions of the sky!
—Lucretius, *De Rerum Natura* 1.1038–1039[1]

In *The Ethics of Ambiguity*, Simone de Beauvoir says that while human life may be spontaneous at its base, it "always projects itself toward something" and is not "an upsurging as stupid as the *clinamen*" (Beauvoir, *Ethics of Ambiguity*, 25). Clinamen is a Latin term that Lucretius coined to mean the unpredictable swerve of atoms that created the universe. According to Beauvoir, human life may be spontaneous in its "originary facticity", but when it comes to meaning and responsibility, such spontaneity ultimately falls aside in light of how we orient ourselves toward our futures (e.g., our projects, plans, or being with others in the world). For Beauvoir, the principles of human life thus parallel the principles of the universe: "it was quite necessary for the atom to arrive somewhere" (15), she says, as each person arrives at a unique future. So, while human existence may spring forth from pure contingency, such contingency demands a response from beings in the world and can't maintain itself as original spontaneity—it is *up to us* to determine where we want to go and who we want to be. Thus Beauvoir concludes that we must decide whether to embrace our freedom and the responsibility that accompanies it, or whether we want to surrender it, choosing instead to be as stupid as the clinamen.

Of course, we can err. In fact, as we know from Aristotle's *Nicomachean Ethics*, to err is easy, but to hit the mark is most difficult, particularly regarding ethical action. The same goes for Beauvoir: We are spontaneously cast into the world, and our responsibility lies in our choosing to make meaning in this world or not. For Beauvoir, then, while our chance springing into the world may be what has happened to happen, our lives are very much—if not entirely—chosen, and thus are almost completely up to us. *We* decide; *we* choose; *we* embrace our freedom or choose to ignore it. The burden of our existence is completely on, and for, us.

Following these thoughts from Beauvoir, this paper engages the relationship among human responsibility, error, and our place in the cosmos

---

1   The 1987 Englert translation of the *De Rerum Natura* is used throughout.
Complete information for all references can be found in the Select Bibliography at the end of this essay.

---

through accounts of chance and the clinamen in Lucretius's *On The Nature Of Things* (*De Rerum Natura*) and Spinoza's *Theological-Political Treatise* and his *Short Treatise*. Specifically, the question is: How does the affirmation or denial of chance as a metaphysical or existential principle determine how we think of human responsibility and error, particularly regarding how we can err in interpreting the nature of the universe? What we shall see is that an affirmation of chance, when considered in light of the cosmic underpinnings of Lucretius's clinamen, offers a compelling counterpoint to the privation of chance in Spinoza, for whom chance signifies either a lack of understanding of the causes of things or superstitious beliefs. In fact, for Lucretius, our human ability to interpret the universe—from its origins to our ethical decisions—paradoxically *depends* on a chance swerve.

The first section of this paper explains the twofold role of chance in Lucretius's poem (i.e., as the clinamen, a chance swerve that creates the universe; and as the explanation for the ways in which we interpret the nature of this universe, both truly and in error). The second section explains Spinoza's rejection of chance and the reasons why it holds no place in the universe, either as a cosmic principle or as an explanation of how we human beings err in our interpretations of the universe. In the third and final section I argue that we ought to prefer Lucretius's thinking about chance to Spinoza's, at least insofar as existential principles are concerned. In that section we will also see how Lucretius's thinking directly influences and resonates with some contemporary philosophers (for my purposes, Jacques Derrida and Georges Bataille) who regard the existence of chance as *necessary* for human experience and philosophical investigation. Thus, by turning to Lucretius and making a detour through Spinoza, we will see not only how chance functions for both philosophers, but also how Beauvoir's thinking betrays an underlying prejudice with an overarching downfall: We human beings may in fact be as stupid as the clinamen, but maybe the clinamen isn't so stupid after all.

I. LUCRETIUS'S AFFIRMATION OF CHANCE

For Lucretius, chance is of two orders. The first order is a cosmological principle of creation, without which "nature never would have created anything" (2.224); the second order of chance pertains to how we interpret the nature of the universe, an interpretation that itself is a creative activity. The first principle of creation is the chance swerve, or clinamen, which is something that just moves slightly off a determined course to create something else—in this case, the whole universe. Without this movement, the universe never would have come into being:

> Unless [atoms] were accustomed to swerving, all would fall downwards like drops of rain through the deep void. [2.222–223]

Without the swerve, nothing could ever have come into being, nor continue to be. Interesting to note in this passage is how Lucretius speaks of atoms being *accustomed* to such events: Part of what it means to be an atom entails nonlinear activity, or activity that seems to be *against* the nature of an atom.

To understand the force of this statement, consider an analogy to Aristotle's thinking about ethical activity throughout his *Nicomachean Ethics*. Aristotle maintains that an individual must change personal habits in order to become good or virtuous, because human beings are not simply good by nature. For Aristotle, changing one's habits is the key to changing one's nature. Good habits don't come naturally; rather, a person must strive to change habits *in order to* affect his or her nature—a distinction remains between what occurs by nature and what occurs in other ways. Yet, the nature of a human life or any other kind of being recognizes the potential *of* that life. Thus for Aristotle, habits don't simply occur by nature or against it, but unfold from the potential of a human life to change its very existence. Otherwise, human beings too would be like atoms in a void: all necessity, with no change, and no creativity.

This analogy to Aristotelian ethical activity points out that what it means to become "accustomed" to something belongs to the nature of a given being but does so in a way that signifies something other than a mere unfolding of a thing's essential properties in a determined and calculable manner. Lucretius's chance swerve demonstrates this point well. Explanations of the creation of the universe that imply divine origins or pure necessity, Lucretius says, fail because

> This world was made *by nature*, and the seeds
> of things, colliding *on their own*, automatically, by chance, were driven
> together in many ways, senselessly, purposelessly, vainly.
> But at last those seeds coalesced which, *suddenly thrown together*,
> might on each occasion become the beginnings of great things:
> of the world, sea, sky, and the race of living creatures.
> [2.1057–1063, emphasis mine)]

That is, this contingent activity fixes the center of Lucretius's universe, generating the whole of it, even "great things", and does so by nature. Incidental relationships, one might say, aren't so incidental to Lucretius.

If the possibility of a chaotic element at the core of Lucretius's cosmos has traction, and if one agrees that purposeless activity accounts for generation and growth from the incidental collision of atoms or seeds, then what might one make of the place of human beings in this universe, or of the nature of the human mind? Vain action does not seem to be the norm for human life; rather, realizing one's purposeful or necessary activity in one's mind seems to demonstrate the opposite point. Yet for Lucretius,

the mind itself
has no internal necessity in performing all its actions,
and is not forced as if conquered to bear and suffer,
the tiny swerve of the atoms. [2.289–292]

That is, just as no necessary causal relationship among all beings (on account of the force of contingency in the universe) exists in a universally regulated way, so too does no one action or way of being result from an internal mental necessity. The human mind, then, is like the universe insofar as it also manifests activity based on a multitude of potential, and even a chance swerve fails to dictate what a mind will do.

Yet this point deserves more consideration, for while the nature of the swerve itself seems to receive the most attention from scholars, in Lucretius's poem the relationship among the swerve and human action, activity, and freedom is controversial: What is the relationship between the chance motions of the universe and human action? Consider what Tim O'Keefe says: "Lucretius' description of the swerve tells us remarkably little about the role it is supposed to play in preserving our freedom" (*Epicurus on Freedom*, 26). Stating his case more firmly, O'Keefe also says:

> The swerve is *not* involved directly in the production of free
> action; it is *not* supposed to secure the agent as the *archē*
> [origin] of either his character or his actions; it is *not* needed
> to protect the emergent self from the threat of reductionism.
> [123]

Because it is an *archē* of collisions that generates the universe, human beings are removed from such concerns; our minds, rather than a chance swerve, carry us where we want to go because we desire certain pleasures (31). The mind, then, moves itself independently from the rest of the universe.

Against this reading of the separation between human action and chance swerves, Walter Englert argues that the swerve "is the source of motion within us, and is involved in every action" (*Epicurus on the Swerve*, 66). Locating the *archē kinēseōs* (origin of motion) within human beings as much as in the whole of the cosmos, the swerve thus initiates the whole of motion for all creatures, from our bodies to our minds; everything is bound to the motions of the swerve as it originates both externally to human beings and internally as well. Englert thus says that Lucretius argues,

> in the form of a *reductio ad absurdum* [...] that if the swerve
> does not exist, we cannot explain why living creatures have
> the power to move when they want, i.e., why they seem to
> have the source of motions within them". [66]

Thus, according to Englert, the very principles of the universe that set it in motion likewise apply to all creatures, including human beings: "The main thrust of the Lucretius passage is to show how the swerve accounts for voluntary action in general, not the more narrow class of actions for which human beings are morally responsible" (143). The chance swerve, then, may provide an explanation for the movement of the cosmos (be it purely physical or entailing a mental component), and is necessarily replicated throughout the whole of nature and everything in it.

These opposing interpretations point to the ambiguous status of the clinamen in Lucretius's poem, and it seems that either we must take it as inaugurating the whole of nature removed from our place in it on account of the power of the human mind to negate the force of chance, or we must take it as something like a seed implanted in each being to allow for that being's movement and growth.[2] Likely, Beauvoir would concur with O'Keefe's reading of Lucretius: The original spontaneity that cast beings into the world is meaningfully separable from our experience of it, for the mind is at odds with chance happenings as anything other than an *archē* of creation. And while Beauvoir may appreciate Englert's reading of Lucretius insofar as it too says that the clinamen cannot account for human beings' moral responsibility, ultimately Englert's reading offers too strongly a reduction of creativity in the universe, thus failing to satisfy the real ways in which we experience ourselves and our world. Still, we should prefer some aspects of Englert's reading—i.e., that the chance swerve accompanies all of life, human and otherwise—not because it offers a reduction to a basic mechanical principle of the universe, but because it highlights the ways in which Lucretius speaks of chance as operative *in our very investigation* of nature. That is, rather than relying just on a negative reduction of possibilities for the generation of the cosmos that leads to the conclusion that chance encounters must be responsible for it (an idea at which Spinoza will scoff), Lucretius provides another and more remarkable way in which chance is affirmed in his universe—i.e., through its operation in our lives, demonstrated in our attempts to interpret nature.

Less familiar to us than the primary articulation of chance as a cosmologically generative creative swerve, this second order of chance at work in Lucretius's poem is found in his references to how we experience both the universe and the poet's own words, insofar as our own swerving experiences exceed the boundaries of ontological creation and spill instead into the task of interpretation, or how we take up and encounter the flux of the cosmos with us implicated in it. Roughly half of the references to chance in this poem concern themselves with the clinamen or chance swerve, however ambiguous its status

---

2   This latter interpretation may resonate with Spinoza's *conatus*, which is his way of explaining how each being strives to persevere in its being, given the nature that it is. In some ways, Lucretius's universe seems to operate on similar principles.

---

may be, according to the ways in which I discussed the first order of chance. The second references, however, are Lucretius's addresses to "someone", "us", or even to "you", the reader, for when one takes up the task of *interpreting* the creation of the universe, one can go awry. I simply point out the kinds of statements in question here, and will explain the force of them in the third section with the help of Derrida and Bataille, after detailing objections to Lucretius's way of thinking from Spinoza. Important to note, though, is that Lucretius takes chance to be operative not only as the generative principle of nature, but also as being at work in our interpretation of it. To this end, Lucretius's sentences often look like this:

> During his discussion of the void, he says that

> if someone by chance should happen to think that this occurs when the bodies leap apart because the air compresses itself, he errs. [1.391–393]

> He then urges us to "trust in these words" of his (1.401).

> We might "by chance [...] think that souls make their escape" during sleep (4.37), but this would be a grave—though possible—error, according to Lucretius.

> "[I]f by chance you believe that the same things existed before" that exist now (5.338–339), and that there is stasis in the universe, then this is also an error, according to Lucretius.

We can see from these examples (which are a few of many[3]) that Lucretius acknowledges the role of chance when we're engaged in the interpretive task of investigating the universe. However, we do not know how these "errors" occur, i.e., how one can go awry in considering the creation of the cosmos, especially since the cosmos itself, as Lucretius delineates, admits of detours of the clinamen. Are we no part of this creation, insofar as we are human beings who inhabit the very universe in question? And how are we to understand our role in the poem, as Lucretius urges us to trust his words, noting paradoxically throughout, as he does, that words themselves are impoverished (1.138), that we create new words for many things (1.137), and that language must adapt to the changing ways of nature (1.823–833)? Lucretius's emphasis on the possibility of error is helpful for understanding Spinoza's suspicion of chance in the *Theological-Political Treatise* and how we can anticipate a response to Spinoza's

---

3   Other examples include 1.391–393, 1.770–775, 2.37–49, 2.83–87, 3.697–700, 3.818–823, 3.861–865, 4.739–743, 5.110–121, 5.338–344.

---

puzzling indictment of wonder as a kind of error in his *Short Treatise on God, Man, and his Well-Being.*

II. SPINOZA'S REJECTION OF CHANCE

In a letter to Hugo Boxel in which he dismisses the existence of ghosts, Spinoza says, "The authority of Plato, Aristotle, and Socrates carries little weight with me. I should have been surprised if you had produced Epicurus, Democritus, Lucretius or one of the Atomists or defenders of the atoms" (Spinoza, Letter 60, *The Essential Spinoza*, 287). According to Spinoza, the former group (Plato et al.) "invented occult qualities, intentional species, substantial forms, and a thousand other trifles" (ibid), whereas the latter were too busy investigating the true nature of the universe to be bothered with falsities or phantasms of the imagination. But, by writing a cosmological poem in which the universe is based on a chance swerve and human beings ought to pursue desire and pleasure, Lucretius appears to be a perfect foil of Spinoza. Spinoza provides a view of the universe in which everything is well-ordered and every thing has its place; furthermore, human beings ought not pursue pleasure, but intellectual intuition that amounts to understanding the importance of necessity in the universe. Also, Spinoza's main treatise, the *Ethics,* is written in geometrical style—a manner of writing that seems to oppose the very nature of poetry. And we may push the contrast even further. Lucretius writes,

> it is more effective to gauge a person in times
> of doubt and danger, and to learn what they are like in adversity.
> For then at last real voices are extracted from the bottom
> of the heart and the mask is ripped off: reality remains. [3.55–58]

Contrast this statement with Spinoza, for whom doubt—along with error and wonder—are fundamentally privations of knowledge, signifying something that must be actively overcome through the intellect in order to achieve a better understanding of the nature of things. Against the idea of doubt, wonder, and error as mere privations in Spinoza, Lucretius urges us *to* doubt and wonder so that we might see for ourselves the truth *in our very doubting,* which reveals the ways in which the clinamen is operative even in our lives.

In his *Theological-Political Treatise,* Spinoza casts chance and fortune as superstition, not allowing them any place in nature other than rendering them as an excuse for our human inability to manage our own affairs or understand the true nature of the universe.[4] In the preface to this text, Spinoza writes, "If

---

4   Human beings' reliance on miracles receives the same treatment from Spinoza as chance does. For him, miracles are basically a *reductio ad absurdum* explanation of an occurrence such that, when we fail to adequately grasp the cause of something, we call the event "miraculous", when really it's just our inability to truly explain it.

---

men could manage all their affairs by a certain plan [or counsel], or if fortune were always favorable to them, they would never be in the grip of superstition" (*Theological-Political Treatise*, 3.5). But, since "all men by nature are liable to superstition" (3.5), this superstition takes the following form:

> if, while they are tormented by fear, they see something happen which reminds them of some past good or evil, they think that it portends either a fortunate or unfortunate outcome, and for that reason they call it a favorable or unfavorable omen, even though it may deceive them a hundred times. [3.5]

The reason for believing or trusting in chance or fortune, then, is because we generally vacillate between hope and fear, and our "immoderate desire for the uncertain goods of fortune" (3.5) tends, if not to assuage our fears, to give us hope for the future. Such hope for Spinoza, however, seems, in a first gloss, as misplaced as thinking that one can—and will—win the lottery in one's lifetime.

These opening passages demonstrate how chance and fortune both have a stranglehold on our lives (i.e., when things go awry, we hope against hope for something good to come our way), and how our misplaced trust in turns of good fortune ultimately leads to our being deceived about nature. About these lines, Martin Yaffe writes,

> Here is a practical project, to be understood in light of its far-reaching theoretical implications. [...] Spinoza raises the prospect of our having everything we want when and as we want it, and so of achieving complete freedom from worry in our lives. [Yaffe, "Spinoza's *Theologico-Political Treatise*", 113]

But, such freedom from worry is unlikely at best, however much it might realistically occupy our thoughts. Yaffe continues by saying, "what is bad about [superstition] is that it is so deceiving. It deepens our worries instead of lifting them. According to Spinoza, people turn to superstitious behavior out of a mixture of overconfidence and desperation" (Yaffe, 113). In other words, when we long for goods that we can't or don't have, or when we suffer and wish we didn't, then wishing and hoping for good fortune follows from our own deprived state of affairs.[5]

---

5   Spinoza's suspicion of superstition resonates strongly with Lucretius's suspicion of "divine" explanations of the generation of the universe in his poem (cf. *DRN* 1.146–150, 1.930–934). Throughout it, Lucretius constantly dismisses those who would attribute the creation of the universe to divine causes for the sake of human beings, and he too knows that his thoughts may be seen as heretical. The reason for this heresy is due to the fact that Lucretius, in many ways, is engaged in the same

But how can—let alone should—one respond to such openly human concerns? To understand Spinoza in these passages, it might be helpful to pay attention, as we began to do with Lucretius, to how it is that we hear Spinoza's words: *If* human beings could see in advance of themselves, secure certain goods, and achieve soundness of heart, free from worry, *then* trust in chance encounters, reliance on fortune, and, ultimately, belief in superstition wouldn't happen. As counterfactuals, however, "if" and "then" denote wishful thinking: *If* I won the lottery, *then* I wouldn't be writing this paper. Spinoza reminds us that in fact people cannot see far in advance of themselves, and they are not free from worry; consequently, they do have hopes for uncertain futures, they do trust in chance, and they do easily believe in things unseen and unproven. Spinoza's concern in these passages is to find something true in the face of undereducated and mistaken beliefs (a conversation that sustains itself throughout the rest of this text). As Harold Joachim points out, "If [...] we are fully to understand the nature of truth, we must 'deduce' it from the nature of the intellect—the power of clear thinking which generates, and is, all true ideas" (Joachim, *Spinoza's Tractatus*, 154). In his reading, the role of error, like the role of mistaken trust in chance or future prospects, is not

> false thinking, but failure to think or absence of thought; not
> an action, but a passion or obsession of the mind; occurring
> only in regard to objects of imaginational experience, i.e.,
> objects that are, or have been presented to, sense, or are in
> ultimate analysis composed of sensible materials. [166]

The imagination, thus, and everything that it entails in intersecting an individual with the world, passively soaks in what it senses, while the intellect actively corrects what the imagination does not know. Thus, it seems that the mistake we make regarding fortune is that our intellects aren't keen enough and don't know enough not to trust in things that aren't true, either through the deduction of our minds to true ideas, or through the intrinsic nature of the thing itself (in this case, the nature of the universe). The suggestion that follows is that by attending to the light of our intellect, we cannot—*will* not—go astray, for our reason will lead us to the truth of things, or we should see the truth of things through the power of our intellect.

But what do we do with Spinoza on this point, given his usual sensitivity to the particular situations of human beings with our unique affects and aspirations to joy? My suspicion is that in his prefatory remarks, Spinoza speaks less about the truth of beliefs or religious superstition than he does of the true role that chance plays in our lives, if not by some cosmic design then by our

---

process as Spinoza—i.e., a desire to discover the underlying structures of nature, however different they ultimately may appear from Spinoza's investigation of them.

understanding of the world around us through our affects and imaginations. Moira Gatens and Genevieve Lloyd respond to real hopes and fears and their role in Spinoza's thinking by saying,

> where the Stoics saw hope and fear as resting on false beliefs about the importance of what lies beyond human control, and freedom as residing in a retreat to reason, Spinoza's way of 'conquering fortune' rests on the use of reason to understand the operations of imagination and the passions. His version of the life of reason acknowledges the inevitability of hope and fear, along with the other passions. The power of reason resides not in shedding them but in understanding them and, to that extent, becoming free. [Gatens and Lloyd, *Collective Imaginings*, 32]

That is, if we can understand how fortune and chance operate in human life, then we can be free from our indebtedness to them by virtue of the power of the intellect.

Such a premise sounds promising: Simply understand the ways in which we can't see in advance of ourselves, that we only wish good things for ourselves through the imagination and the passions, not the light of reason, and we can free ourselves from the shackles of chance, thereby gaining control of our lives, or at least warding off deceit. For Gatens and Lloyd, "Fickle fortune and implacable fate both dissolve in the reintegration of reason, imagination and emotion", for fortune and fate are "the real operations of imagination and affect in human life" (*Collective Imaginings*, 65). Through the interplay of reason (which attends to the truth of things), imagination (which itself contains no error), and emotion (which tells us ways in which we are affected by the world), we can see chance for what it is: a privation of knowledge about the truth of things.

This understanding may be so. It could be that our dependence on wishful thinking arises through our inability to understand the world around us through the keen use of our intellect or reason, or it may be that our hopes for good turns of fortune arise from a deeply-rooted need to alleviate the worries that we have in life. However, what troubles me in Spinoza's words is not only his thinking about how we mistakenly trust in things that we don't or can't know (e.g., what will happen to us in the future, or why it is that we've suffered as we have), but that Spinoza seems to trust what we can't see or know in other ways. (I have in mind here Spinoza's letter to Oldenburg in which he says that while he can't "prove" that the universe and our human roles in it are akin to the relationship between the worm and the blood, he is led to believe that our relationship is similar to what the worm itself sees: We must trust in *something* in order to get to the truth of things.[6])

---

6   In this letter (Letter 32), Spinoza explains that our human place in the universe is

Most perplexing to this end (i.e., how it is that we come to have knowledge about the universe at all) are Spinoza's statements about wonder and how it, too, signifies a lack of knowledge. In the *Short Treatise on God, Man, and his Well-Being*, Spinoza writes,

> Many Philosophers must also be like that. They have deluded themselves into thinking that beyond this plot of ground, or little globe, on which they are, there is nothing more (because they have seen nothing else). But there is no wonder in him who draws true conclusions. [*Short Treatise*, 100]

In this passage, wonder may go either way: Either those who fail to see beyond themselves have no wonder because they are mistakenly convinced that their "plot of ground" is all that there is (and thus wonder may be a positive moment for these people), or wonder is to be disparaged in favor of a kind of certainty drawn from true conclusions, from what the intellect alone can deduce and reason. A few passages later, Spinoza seems to prefer the latter reading, saying that wonder "arises either from ignorance or from prejudice [and] is an imperfection in the man who is subject to this emotion". Though Spinoza qualifies this statement and says that wonder is simply an "imperfection" because wonder "through itself does not lead to any evil" (*Short Treatise*, 104), and thus is not itself evil, he nonetheless maintains that it serves as a reminder that one who wonders is not experiencing joy (as it is deemed in the *Short Treatise*), or happiness (as it is called in the *Treatise on the Emendation of the Intellect*), or the unification of the intellect with the whole of nature. Wonder, in this sense, is a kind of error that must be overcome in order to get to the truth of the matter.

And so we have at least two ways in which human beings err: either through mistakenly placing trust in things like chance and good fortune, which lead to superstitious beliefs that are dangerous because they deceive us into thinking things true or possible when they're not; or through the act of wondering, which also denotes a lack of knowledge or keenness of intellect. If we depend on unforeseen things or turns of events, then we err; if we wonder, then we don't know the true state of affairs and our intellect is impoverished.

---

akin to a worm's place in blood: While we can't get an entire picture of the whole universe because our perspectives are limited in the way that a worm is limited by its perspective in blood, we can use our reason to guide us in our investigations. In that way, we are like a worm in blood insofar as we are limited by our own perspectives, but unlike a worm, we have reason. For Spinoza, reason gives us hope that we might come to know the whole of nature, even though reason itself can't guarantee such knowledge: "As to knowing the actual manner of this coherence and the agreement of each part with the whole, I made it clear in my previous letter that this is beyond my knowledge" (*Essential Spinoza*, p. 269).

Hence we encounter human beings as privations of intellect, for surely most of us don't in fact know the true nature of the universe or even our place in it.

At times, though, Spinoza signifies that he is not immune to hope and error, try though he might to resist them in his quest for a good that leads to "joy to eternity". In the *Treatise on the Emendation of the Intellect* he describes his task to reach a certain good and how it is that he must relinquish certain evils as follows:

> For I saw that my situation was one of great peril and that I was obliged to seek a remedy with all my might, however uncertain it might be, like a sick man suffering from a fatal malady who, foreseeing certain death unless a remedy is forthcoming, is forced to seek it, however uncertain it be, with all his might, for therein lies all his hope. [*Treatise*, 165]

I do not take this moment in Spinoza to be simply poetic; rather, it aptly responds to the very human situation in which we find ourselves. That is, even Spinoza hopes against hope for a remedy, however uncertain it may be, for what ails him. He does not decide the nature of this remedy any more than he ensures that one exists for him; rather, hope itself propels him to find an end.

We might be tempted to say that this passage demonstrates a trust in something unseen or unproven in our experience, like a reliance on chance or the experience of wonder. In this way, then, we might be tempted to hold Spinoza accountable for what he simply does not know: how it is that we seek out remedies for what ails us, conscientious of our over-reliance on things that remain unseen to us, warding against failure and error at every turn.

Or, we might return to Lucretius. If he is right in saying that it is effective to gauge a person's character in times of doubt and danger, for in these moments people are uncovered and reveal their true identities, then we might be able to resist readings of Spinoza that demand perfection from us and nothing else. Spinoza sees himself in danger, and the moments in which we hope for good things and fear that they may not happen might not be too far from Spinoza's own experience, for we, too, see ourselves in danger and hope, with all our might, to find a remedy as well.

III. CONTEMPORARY PHILOSOPHICAL SUPPORT OF LUCRETIUS

Lucretius, whom Spinoza admires because of his atomistic conception of the whole of nature, offers a view of chance that holds both metaphysical and existential implications, a view that itself exceeds a simple reduction of chance to atomistic principles. Spinoza's interest in Lucretius does not attend to these non-atomistic principles insofar as chance is concerned, though, because any consideration of "chance" in Spinoza betrays his conception of a necessarily well-ordered universe. That is, the validation of chance, according to Spinoza, either in one's thinking (wherein chance signifies an inability to understand the nature of things, or a reliance on superstitious thinking) or as the foundation of the universe (as a swerve, the clinamen, a happening or an event) cannot be admitted. For Spinoza, it *is* possible to accurately understand, through the hard work of the intellect, how *everything* is necessarily how and as it is. The failure to do so would be ours, and would have nothing to do with chance.

Yet before acquiescing to Spinoza's objections to chance, further consideration of Lucretius's concept of the role of chance in interpreting nature brings to mind the work of contemporary philosophers Jacques Derrida and Georges Bataille.

In his lecture-essay, "My Chances/*Mes Chances*: A Rendezvous with Some Epicurean Stereophonies", Derrida says,

> Dasein's [Being's] chances are, in the first place and also, its falls.
> And they are always mine, *mes chances*, each time related to its
> relation to itself. [Dasein, in being thrown, is then] originarily
> abandoned to fall and decline or, we could say, to chance. [9]

Here, Derrida signifies that chance involves a downward movement, an experience of something falling upon us from above, such that our sense of horizon—or the horizon that we *thought* we knew—becomes destabilized until a certain other ground smacks our face as we ourselves are forced to fall. Derrida wonders if our attention is engaged, then, *by* the ground or the abyss, and one must wonder if this is the case indeed, if thinking and experience and life might be a series of falls, not from some revered place like Milton's paradise, but a continuum of falls, one replacing the other.

Derrida reminds us that these chances are ours, and ours alone. To this end, Derrida says,

> One can fall well or badly, have a lucky or unlucky break—but
> always by dint of not having foreseen—of not having seen in
> advance and ahead of oneself. In such a case, when man or
> the subject falls, the fall affects his upright stance and vertical
> position by engraving in him the detour of a *clinamen*, whose
> effects are sometimes inescapable. [5]

As a generative principle, the clinamen is blind, unknowing, and acts in vain: but we should recall that for Lucretius, the clinamen is the very possibility of the creation in the first place, and the detours that we experience are contours within this very universe. For this reason, the clinamen resonates with how we experience ourselves *in* the universe, not separate from it.

Derrida is keen on this point and thus directs our attention to the disorientation we experience within a given horizon, noting the severe vertigo—

utter vertical disequilibrium—that we experience when "*oevres* befall us". He says that *oevres*—openings, gashes, chasms—"speak about or unveil that which falls *in* its befalling upon us. They overpower us inasmuch as they explain themselves with that which falls from above" (17). Rather than being a straight fall into a vacuum-esque abyss, Derrida reminds us that, like the swerve or clinamen itself (or like the tower of Pisa), "[t]he *oevre* is vertical and slightly leaning" (17). The slight lean of the opening itself resists the gravity, as it were, of the situation: In this moment, freedom of thought, like the very generation of the cosmos, for Lucretius, is possible. And how? Lucretius reminds us that

> it is necessary to admit that what existed before has perished
> and what exists now was created now. [3.677–679]

The force of creation persists in the present, and as I have submitted, in our experiences and interpretative tasks. After all, if the *oevre* itself is both vertical and leaning, then the horizon for thinking, interpreting, and experiencing the world must similarly be askew (if not always anew). Derrida reminds us that our language even permits of such experience: recall that the words "chance" and "cadence" descend to us from *cadere*, the Latin word which simply means "to fall".[7]

For Derrida, this thinking culminates in our inability to anticipate, to see or grasp in advance that which might befall us. There is a certain risk indeed to opening oneself to the possibility of *oevres*, a certain risk in throwing oneself and one's words to an unknown audience, say. Yet we *take our chances*, though this statement itself might suggest that we can grasp the very opening of the horizon as it befalls us before we experience it, that we may, in taking chances, grasp Walt Whitman's "gossamer thread" where it lands.

In *Guilty*, Georges Bataille echoes these thoughts from Derrida. He says, "The human mind is set up to take no account of chance, except insofar as the calculations that eliminate chance allow you to forget it: that is, *not take it into account*" (Bataille, *Guilty*, 71). This point is clear, Derrida might say, when we demand reasons for every event—a demand with which Spinoza would surely agree. Yet *not* taking chance into account, for Bataille as for Derrida, would be an error. Condemning both philosophical reflection and mindless repetition, Bataille says, "All philosophy [...] is reflection on a lifeless residue, on a regular process that allows neither chance nor mischance. To recognize chance is a suicide of knowledge"; nonetheless it is "concealed in a philosopher's despair" (*Guilty*, 77). That is, ever at work at the center of all thought is chance, threatening to topple philosophical systems and disrupt our routines.

---

7   This word is akin to the etymology of the word "accident" from the Greek phrase *kata symbēbēkos*, which means "to fall together".

Yet for Bataille, chance as an existential reality is key. In speaking of a person chancing to fall off a building, and while falling, catching a hook on the side of that building, thus arresting the fall, Bataille says,

> I understand now—picturing the momentum of falling—that there's nothing in this world unless it meets up with a *hook*. Usually we avoid seeing a hook. We confer an aspect of necessity on ourselves, on the universe, on the earth, on people. [74]

For these reasons, we don't admit of chance encounters. Derrida speaks of Dasein's chances as falling to us from above yet belonging to us alone. Bataille reminds us in the passage to remain open to the world because one never knows when one might find a hook. In both, the force of the existential aspects of thinking about change is clear: Chance allows us ways of speaking and thinking about the life of the universe as we are bound to it, and as we try to interpret it. The act of interpretation demands openness to this universe, and to our nature. This openness follows Aristotle's insistence that we must try to change our habits in order to change our nature. This openness also follows Lucretius, who recognizes that our nature already contains the power to be changed. And Bataille concurs:

> Man reads the possible outline of chance in his 'customs,' an outline that is himself, a state of grace, an arrow let fly. Animals were a wager, and so is man, we're an arrow released into air. Where it will fall, I can't say. Where I'll fall, I can't say. [Bataille, 77]

In other words, while one might not achieve the apex of intellectual clarity systematically desired by Spinoza, one might risk such totalizing systemization in order to cultivate a radical openness to the universe and to oneself.

Lucretius is quite aware throughout his poem of the dangers involved in thinking for oneself, or of taking chances. In the beginning of his poem, he says:

> I am afraid of one thing in all of this: that you might think
> that you are starting on the first steps of an unholy system
> of thought,
> and are walking the path of a crime. [1.80–82]

This is why, a bit later, he hedges his bets, saying that

> these little traces are enough for a keen intellect,
> and by their means you are able to discover the rest on your
> own. [1.402–403]

These little traces—are they sufficient for one intellect, however keen it might be? Perhaps we are able to "discover the rest on [our] own" if we heed the advice of Derrida in taking our chances, aware of the possibility of going awry, but conscientious nonetheless of falling through the horizon of thought, and give ourselves over to the disorienting instability of a horizon for thinking. After all, there are not two distinct horizons in which we operate, one that's a cumulative ontology of the universe, and the other that's merely our interpretation of it. Instead, as the creation of the cosmos for Lucretius is itself bound to a fall, or to chance, and insofar as we ourselves experience ourselves, on account of chance, going awry from time to time, creativity and experience themselves entail at least the detour of the clinamen. If we are to create or discover anything, then, according to Lucretius and Derrida, we must risk stability, take our chances, and realize, as Derrida does, that there is only "verticality and the unforeseeable" ("My chances", 6)—i.e., the so-called "stupidity" of the clinamen.

SELECT BIBLIOGRAPHY

Bataille, Georges. *Guilty*. Translated by Bruce Boone. Venice: The Lapis Press, 1988.

Beauvoir, Simone de. *The Ethics of Ambiguity*. Translated by B. Frechtman. New York: Citadel Press, 2000.

Derrida, Jacques. "My Chances / *Mes Chances*: A rendezvous with some Epicurean stereophonies". In *Taking Chances: Derrida, Psychoanalysis, and Literature*. Edited by Joseph H. Smith and William Kerrigan. Baltimore: Johns Hopkins University Press, 1984.

Englert, Walter. *Epicurus on the Swerve and Voluntary Action*. Atlanta: Scholars Press, 1987.

Gatens, Moira, and Genevieve Lloyd. *Collective Imaginings: Spinoza Past and Present*. New York: Routledge, 1999.

Joachim, Harold H. *Spinoza's Tractatus de Intellectus Emendatione: A Commentary*. Bristol: Thoemmes Press, 1993. Originally published Oxford: Clarendon Press, 1940.

Lucretius. *On the Nature of Things*. Translated by Walter Englert. Newburyport: Focus Publishing/R. Pullins Company, 2003.

O'Keefe, Tim. *Epicurus on Freedom*. New York: Cambridge University Press, 2005.

Spinoza, Benedict de. *The Collected Works of Spinoza*, vol. 1. Edited and translated by Edwin Curley. Princeton: Princeton University Press, 1985.

———. *The Letters*. Translated by Samuel Shirley. Indianapolis: Hackett Publishing Company, 1995.

———. *Short Treatise on God, Man, and His Well-Being*. In *The Collected Works*, vol. 1. Edited and translated by Edwin Curley. Princeton: Princeton University Press, 1985.

———. "A Critique of Traditional Religion", part of *Theological-Political Treatise*. In *A Spinoza Reader: The* Ethics *and Other Texts*. Edited and translated by Edwin Curley. Princeton: Princeton University Press, 1994.

———. *Treatise on the Emendation of the Intellect*. In *A Spinoza Reader: The* Ethics *and other Texts*. Edited and translated by Edwin Curley. Princeton: Princeton University Press, 1994.

———. *The Essential Spinoza:* Ethics *and Related Writings*. Edited by Michael Morgan, translated by Samuel Shirley. Indianapolis: Hackett Publishing Company, 2006.

Yaffe, Martin D. "Spinoza's *Theologico-Political Treatise*—A First Inside Look". In *Piety and Humanity: Essays on Religion and Early Modern Political Philosophy*, edited by Douglas Kries, 109–134. Lanham, Maryland: Rowman & Littlefield, 1997.

"HALF BURIED … / OR FANCY-BOURNE": UNEARTHED DESIRES AND THE FAILURE OF TRANSCENDENCE IN TENNYSON'S "LUCRETIUS"

Vincent Bissonette

In December of 1865, Alfred Tennyson (1809–1892) had dinner with the politician William Gladstone, the Pre-Raphaelite artists William Holman Hunt and Thomas Woolner, and the senior John Addington Symonds. After dinner, Symonds's son, also John Addington, joined them. Finding the company still seated around the dining table and finishing dessert, the young critic, then in his 20s, "relapsed into an armchair between Woolner and my father" (Symonds, *Letters*, 1).[1] In his journal account of the evening, he writes that he "was like a man hearing a concerto", the main players being Gladstone ("first violin") and Tennyson ("violincello") (4). The conversation ranged from the recent and brutal suppression of rebellion in Jamaica and the imminent Reform Bill of 1867 to Huxley's claim that humans descend from monkeys and questions on the relation between morality and immortality. Throughout his account Symonds focuses on the disagreements between Tennyson and Gladstone:

> Gladstone arguing, Tennyson putting in a prejudice; Gladstone asserting rashly, Tennyson denying with a bald negative; Gladstone full of facts, Tennyson relying on impressions; both of them humorous, but the one polished and delicate in repartee, the other broad and coarse and grotesque. Gladstone's hands are white and not remarkable. Tennyson's are huge, unwieldy, fit for moulding clay or dough. Gladstone is in some sort a man of the world; Tennyson a child, and treated by him like a child. [4]

Tennyson's political positions repeatedly shock: For example, he excuses brutality in Jamaica against the "savage mob" and grimly suggests, "If they shot paupers, perhaps they wouldn't tear up their clothes" (4). Then, when the extension of the franchise comes up, he disclaims any knowledge about it, professes that "a state in which every man would have a vote is the ideal", and dismisses the whole thing by asking, "But how to do it?" Never mind the contradiction between these democratic ideals and the earlier remark about shooting paupers. Symonds simply comments, "This was the mere reflector. The man of practice [Gladstone] said nothing" (3–4).

---

1   Complete bibliographic information for all sources can be found in the Select
    Bibliography at the end of this essay.

Symonds is obviously troubled by Tennyson's prejudice and ignorance, but what's most interesting is that he connects it to the poet's status as a "reflector". One of the definitions of *reflection* is "the action of turning (back) or fixing the thoughts on some subject; meditation, deep or serious consideration".[2] When we reflect on something we take the time to judge carefully. Tennyson, however, hardly seems to think but rather to *reflect* passively contemporary contradictions and prejudices.[3] Symonds would later describe the "power of reflection" as a way to "amuse ourselves here [on earth?] with manifold toys", the value of which is "in regard to the comfort and well-being of the individual" (172). Conspicuously absent from this definition is the notion that reflection does or can lead to truth. Rather, it is a way of getting along in the world; it helps us to cope. That, however, seems ill-suited to Tennyson, the poet-laureate of England who pronounces on national matters and mingles with ministers of state. Gladstone's practical knowledge is by far superior.

However, Symonds does not always view Tennyson's reflections as "mere", especially as they turn to more philosophical questions. He still refers to Tennyson's "metaphysical vagueness" as "almost childish" (6). It is the stuff that undergraduates talk about late into the night: Would I show courage in war? In a sudden panic? What if I had an hour to think about it?[4] What is a brick? Do I really have a clear idea of a brick? Can I sympathize with a brick and all its atoms

---

2   *Oxford English Dictionary*, 2nd ed., s.v. "reflection", def. 8. Note also in Lockean epistemology, reflection, along with sensation, is one of the two sources of all ideas (Locke, *Essay*, Book 2, Chapter 1, Section 2; 104).

3   In *The Victorian Age in Literature*, G. K. Chesterton refers to these contradictions and prejudices as the Victorian Compromise, and explains that "Tennyson did sincerely believe in the Victorian compromise; and sincerity is never undignified. […] Tennyson is the exquisitely ornamental extinguisher of the flame of the first revolutionary poets. England has settled down; England has become Victorian. The compromise was interesting, it was national and for a long time it was successful: there is still a great deal to be said for it. But it was as freakish and unphilosophic, as arbitrary and untranslatable, as a beggar's patched coat or a child's secret language" (Chesterton, *Victorian Age*, 162).

4   "The question of his personal courage came up. That, said Gladstone, did not prove his capability of remaining cool under and dealing with such special circumstances. Anecdotes about sudden panics were related. Tennyson said to my father, 'As far as I know my own temperament, I could stand any sudden thing, but give me an hour to reflect, and I should go here and go there, and all would be confused. If the fiery gulf of Curtius opened in the City, I would leap at once into it on horseback. But if I had to reflect on it, no—especially the thought of death— nothing can be weighed against that. It is the moral question, not the fear, which would perplex me. I have not got the English courage. I could not wait six hours in a square expecting a battery's fire'" (Symonds, *Letters*, 2–3).

better than I can with God? What happens when I pray?[5] Symonds is too guarded to enter fully into these reflections, but he nonetheless admires Tennyson for them. He writes, "Tennyson has a perfect simplicity about him which recognises the real greatness of such questions, and regards them as always worthy of consideration. He treats them with profound moral earnestness" (6–7).[6]

Thus, we can see how Symonds's complex sketch places the poet in a certain class of Victorian gentleman—self-satisfied, complacent, provincial, and jingoistic—yet also suggests, in the words G. K. Chesterton, that "the sea of Tennyson's mind was troubled under its serene surface" (*Victorian Age*, 64). The implications of British colonialism, the increasing democratization in England, a materialistic universe: all these threaten the order of Victorian Britain. Gladstone seems in control of himself, if not of the chaotic reality, but Tennyson is all agitation. As Symonds and Chesterton both suggest, this discontent was vital to his poetic achievement.

I want to claim that such anxieties as these and the attempt to tranquilize them are at the thematic core of the dramatic monologue "Lucretius", which Tennyson had begun working on in October 1865 and published in *Macmillan's Magazine* in May 1868. Tennyson is seldom considered a philosophical poet, but I think in this poem he explores sensitively the attraction, the cost, and the fundamental impossibility of tranquility, for the Epicurean philosopher or the Victorian gentleman. Tranquility, in Tennyson's poem, is not merely a hypothetical ideal—something that he might concede as desirable yet dismiss by asking, "But how to do it?" It is rather the object of an obsessive and erotic quest. Indeed, we can only understand the oft-mentioned sexual eroticism of the poem by considering it in relation to Lucretius's erotic relationship towards Epicurus, the gods, and tranquility. Finding in Lucretius something that is finally very un-Epicurean, Tennyson figures the ideal of tranquility as sublimated desire and life-denying obsession.

*

Though Tennyson may have studied *De Rerum Natura* as a boy, his occasion for writing "Lucretius" was almost certainly the 1864 edition of

---

5   "Then about matter. Its incognisability puzzled him. 'I cannot form the least notion of a brick. I don't know what it is. It's no use talking about atoms, extension, colour, weight. I cannot penetrate the brick. But I have far more distinct ideas of God, of love and such emotions. I can sympathise with God in my poor way. The human soul seems to me always in some way, how we do not know, identical with God. That's the value of prayer. Prayer is like opening a sluice between the great ocean and our little channels'" (Symonds, *Letters*, 5–6).

6   Cf. Chesterton, *Victorian Age*, 163: "We cannot help feeling that Tennyson is the Englishman taking himself seriously—an awful sight."

Lucretius published by his friend Hugh Munro, who checked Tennyson's poem and found "that everything [in it] was Lucretian".[7] In its final version, "Lucretius" is 280 lines, almost 250 of which comprise a long monologue by Lucretius that skillfully incorporates quotations, paraphrases, and stylistic elements of *De Rerum Natura*.[8] More significant, though, is Tennyson's use of the old story that Lucretius's wife gave him a love philter that, contrary to her intentions, drove him insane and led to his suicide. This story is first recorded, and perhaps invented, by Jerome, who uses it primarily to undermine Epicurean ethics.[9] As A. A. Markley writes, Tennyson uses it as "a provocative starting point with which to frame his own statement on classical rationalism and its uses in the modern world" (Markley, *Stateliest*, 141). Specifically, the story helps him to raise concerns about the extent to which rationalism—or 19th-century utilitarianism or positivism, for that matter—denies the full range of human emotion, in particular erotic and sexual passions. This suggests the cost of Epicurean tranquility. But even more fundamentally, the poem radically questions the ideal of a human life that escapes the vagaries of chance or accident, which is exactly what the godlike state of Epicurean tranquility seems to promise. Tennyson uses Jerome's story, above all, to insist on Lucretius's human vulnerability to the actions of others, to unforeseen consequences, to unruly human passions, and to madness.

Tennyson's personal life testified to human vulnerability. He was well aware of how his father's life had been ruined by being disinherited, and later he suffered the untimely death of his intimate friend Arthur Hallam (Ricks, *Tennyson*, 1–39, 99–145). Symonds's sketch further suggests that he felt the

---

7 Markley, *Stateliest Measures*, 140; Tennyson, "Lucretius" headnote.

8 One of the most striking features of "Lucretius" is Tennyson's extraordinary incorporation of *De Rerum Natura* into his poem. Almost since its first publication, critics have noticed the "poet's subtle blending of Lucretius's turns of phrases and dozens of details borrowed from his scientific and philosophical tenets" (Markley, *Stateliest*, 141; see also Jebb, Allen, Mustard, Wilner). The amalgam of Tennyson and Lucretius has yielded some interesting critical descriptions. Vance writes, "Tennyson's seemingly random jumbling together of small fragments of Lucretius' text to form his own counter-text wickedly mimes the random collision of Lucretian atoms which forms the Lucretian universe" (Vance, *Victorians*, 109). In contrast, Linda K. Hughes argues that Tennyson's text is "not a mere pastiche of translated quotations lifted from *De Rerum Natura*, but what almost seems a metempsychosis of Lucretius into Tennyson, who is able to embody Lucretius's own psychological associations as revealed in the Latin poem" (Hughes, *Manyfacèd Glass*, 227).

9 *De Rerum Natura*, Loeb edition, xxi. For an extended discussion of the story's merit, see xviii–xxvi; see also Nussbaum, *Therapy* 140–144, where she argues that the story, although generally discredited, has continued to guide readings of Lucretius's treatment of love.

vulnerability of England itself. Throughout that sketch, we can read Tennyson as continually attempting to distance himself from the latter through, for example, a humor that Symonds finds "broad and coarse and grotesque" (*Letters*, 4). Tennyson hardly achieves tranquility in these attempts, but I do think that tranquility is in some sense his objective. In his poem, Tennyson puts forward Lucretius as an altogether more philosophical exemplar of tranquility, though one who fails just as certainly as Tennyson himself, and more tragically.

At the opening of Tennyson's poem, we are told that Lucretius spends his days

> Half buried in some weightier argument,
> Or fancy-borne perhaps upon the rise
> and roll of the Hexameter.   (Tennyson, "Lucretius", 9–11)

Significantly, this intellectual activity is ambiguously characterized as being either "half buried" or "fancy-borne", suggesting a tension between philosophical argument and poetic composition. The monologue, spoken in the calm after a tempestuous night, suggests that philosophy, in hewing to a rational and scientific view of the universe, represses or *buries* the passions (especially erotic passions) that are unearthed in poetry. As Lucretius reflects on his nightmares and attempts to view them in relation to his philosophical project, he becomes increasingly aware of his own unwieldy passions yet stubbornly continues to assert a notion of human dignity in rationalistic terms that deny the passions. Faced with his own animality, he sees suicide as the only manly option:

> Why should I, beastlike as I find myself,
> Not manlike end myself?—our privilege—
> What beast has heart to do it? And what man,
> What Roman would be dragged in triumph thus?
> (Tennyson, 231–234)

In the final lines of his monologue he turns to Tranquility, the "Passionless bride" whom he "woo[s] […] roughly". Literally thrusting the knife into his side, he figuratively rapes Tranquility. The poem ends as his wife rushes onto the scene, her rival Epicurus now supplanted by death. Hysterical, she cries out that she has failed in her duty, to which Lucretius answers, in the poem's final lines:

> Care not thou!
> Thy duty? What is duty? Fare thee well!   (Tennyson, 279–280)

Tennyson thus shows Lucretius involved in an erotics of transcendence. He sublimates sexual desire in order to pursue more worthy pleasures.

Vincent Bissonette

The suicide seems to indicate Tennyson's critique of this path, but before considering that, we need to better appreciate Tennyson's use of Lucretius's text. Though some critics have argued that the poet's Christianity leads him to distort the portrait of the philosopher,[10] just as Jerome had done, I will argue that in dramatizing his (almost certainly fictitious) suicide, Tennyson puts pressure on the tension in Lucretius's philosophy between naturalism and transcendence. Therefore Lucretius's suicide indicates not the failure of his naturalistic philosophy but his failure to give up on transcendence.

*

Certainly, Lucretius subscribed to naturalism and argued that human life was enriched when attempts for transcendence were rejected. In her subtle and attentive reading of Lucretius, Martha Nussbaum describes *De Rerum Natura* as offering a kind of therapy that involves purging the patient of false beliefs, especially those fostered by metaphysics and religion. In Book 4, Lucretius characterizes a man in love as deifying the beloved, desiring to possess completely, and even to devour him or her. Nussbaum's reading shows how Lucretius connects such madness to an erroneous set of beliefs about love—in particular that the lovers become one—that leads one to be "in love" with love (Nussbaum, *Therapy*, 175–176). As Nussbaum describes it, Lucretius leads his reader through a series of arguments meant "to puncture the pretensions of theological and metaphysical explanations of natural conduct and to lead us toward a natural history of the human being" (161). Previous commentators, though they may have been sympathetic to Lucretius's general project, have been unreceptive to his reduction of love. Santayana, for example, "accuses Lucretius of having an impoverished sense of human value because of his negative attitude to love" (Nussbaum, *Therapy*, 143). Nussbaum, however, argues that Lucretius shows us how to keep "the full richness

---

10   Norman Vance writes that Tennyson discredits the "Lucretian system" with
"brilliant unfairness" (*Victorians*, 108). Tennyson uses Lucretius to provide
"imaginative vitality", yet then "asserts the superiority of […] Christian humanism
by maneuvering Lucretian materialism into deconstructing itself—and Lucretius"
(109–110). By turning the poem into the id-like energies of Lucretius opposed
to the superego governing of Christianity, Vance sets up a nice "intellectual
melodrama", as he calls it (108), but I doubt that the poem really works on this
allegorical level. Rather, I am persuaded by Hughes's reading of Tennyson's
sensitivity to the consciousness, intentions, and purposes of his character (Hughes,
Manyfacèd, 227). Where Vance sees Lucretius as a puppet-like figure manipulated
by Tennyson, Hughes sees Tennyson more profoundly entering into Lucretius (or
Lucretius entering into Tennyson). Accordingly, in place of Vance's quasi-objective
concerns with fairness, Hughes leads us to explore Tennyson-Lucretius's relation
to Epicurean philosophy.

of naturalistic explanation—including all the language both physical and psychological, that we would wish to use in talking about ourselves as complex natural beings with a physiology and a mentality that stand in complex relationship to one another" (*Therapy*, 170). In other words, Nussbaum reads Lucretius's project as articulating the utmost value, complexity, and richness of human life precisely in its rejection of religion and metaphysics, with their promise of transcendence, and its adoption of a naturalistic stance that accepts human vulnerability.

However, Lucretius's naturalism is ultimately secondary to his pursuit of the Epicurean ideal of godliness. In her final critique of his views on love, Nussbaum suggests that his goal is not, in the end, naturalism, but rather the "internally godlike" state that Epicureans believed their master had achieved and that they thought attainable to one who had "no deep needs from the world or from one another" (*Therapy*, 190–191). Nussbaum ends her chapter reflecting on this internal contradiction in Lucretius's text:

> In the end, [Lucretius] is an Epicurean, and as an Epicurean, he cannot permit himself, beyond a certain point, to follow his own advice to "yield up to human life." Such neediness before the world would be hateful and terrible to the Epicurean. He does not yield; he demands the life of a self-sufficient god. He says, "I have gotten ahead of you, O Tuchē, and I have built up my fortifications against all your stealthy attacks." Is this the attitude of a cured lover, or is it simply a new form of the disease that Lucretius' therapy was supposed to cure? [191]

In quoting Epicurus's maxim addressed to *Tuchē* (Greek for chance or luck),[11] Nussbaum reminds her readers that, though Epicureans find liberation in naturalism, they also fortify themselves from much that is natural. Nussbaum uses this ethical crux to suggest that what's most valuable in Lucretius is a naturalism allowing for the fullness of human life—including the messiness of

---

11 On *Tuchē*, see Nussbaum's *Fragility of Goodness*, where she uses the term "luck" in a way "closely related to the way in which the Greeks themselves spoke of *tuchē*. I do not mean to imply that the events in question are random or uncaused. What happens to a person by luck will be just what does not happen through his or her own agency, what just *happens* to him, as opposed to what he does or makes. In general, to eliminate luck from human life will be to put that life, or the most important things in it, under the control of the agent (or of those elements in him with which he identifies himself), removing the element of reliance upon the external and undependable" (3–4). *Tuchē* plays a part especially in relation to an individual's dependence on external goods, conflicts between multiple goods, and "ungovernable parts of the human being's internal makeup" such as appetites and desires (6–7). *Fragility* is relevant throughout on this topic.

---

a complicated but not overvalued erotic affair—and not the ideal for Epicurean tranquility that is merely a sublimated desire for transcendence.

*

Nussbaum wants to sort out these strands in Lucretius, but in their entanglement we can connect his project and 19th-century Romanticism, and make sense of Tennyson's reading of his desire for transcendence. Throughout *De Rerum Natura*, Lucretius re-conceptualizes the universe and man's place in it, and one of the ways he does this is through his revisionary view of the gods—and of Epicurus as a god. Infamous atheist though he is, Lucretius frequently invokes the gods, thereby redefining the human relation to the divine. For example, in Book 2 he "appeal[s] to the holy hearts of the gods, which in tranquil peace pass untroubled days and a life serene" (*DRN* 2.1093–1094).[12] Such godliness rests in their complete withdrawal from the world of nature, which is the greatest sign of their wisdom. "Nature", Lucretius writes, "is seen to be free at once and rid of proud masters, herself doing all by her own accord, without the help of the gods" (2.1090–1092). Thus the gods are the opposite of "proud masters". They realize that no one is "strong enough to rule the sum of the immeasurable" or "to hold in hand and control the mighty bridle of the unfathomable" (2.1095–1096). Lucretius follows the Epicurean way because Epicurus was "the first that dared to uplift mortal eyes against [Superstition], the first to make a stand against her; for neither fables of the gods could quell him, nor thunderbolts, nor heaven with menacing roar" (1.66–69). In this enlightened stance, heroism does not involve a struggle with the gods but with superstition.

Paradoxically, however, in rejecting popular fictions about the gods, Lucretius creates a godliness to which humans can aspire. Epicurus is again Lucretius's model. "He was a god", Lucretius writes, "a god he was, who first discovered that reasoned plan of life which is now called Wisdom, who by his skill brought life out of those tempestuous billows and that deep darkness, and settled it in such a calm and in light so clear" (5.8–12). Through "skill", Epicurus found a "plan of life" that made him a god who had "gotten ahead of" *Tuchē*.[13] Perhaps. But, in the light of Jerome's story about Lucretius, this ideal of tranquility and transcendence seems overly optimistic. Certainly it is at odds with the previous deflation of the gods.

These contradictions are recognizable as aspects of the Romantic per-

---

12 The *De Rerum Natura*'s 1992 prose translation by Rouse and Smith (Loeb edition) is used throughout this essay.

13 See Nussbaum, *Fragility*, chapter 4, where she discusses how *technē* (human art or science; =Latin *ars*; =*skill* in the translation above) and "the idea of progress might bring about the elimination of ungoverned contingency from social life" and thus overcome *tuchē* (89).

---

sonality broadly construed: the sense of the universe as uncontrollable and chaotic; the idealization of a godlike serenity; and the human experience of being
planted in the former but longing for the latter.[14] It is not surprising, then, that
in the early 19th century, Lucretius was valued especially for his descriptions of
storms and for his "praise of Epicurus and his lofty project of scientific inquiry
beyond the fiery ramparts of the world" (Vance, *Victorians*, 89). Yet, if many
throughout the 19th century were drawn to his descriptions of chaotic nature
and praise of Epicurus, their attitude toward Lucretius himself was more mixed.
On the one hand, he seemed a gloomy romantic, "associated with depression
and ennui"; while on the other, he was "invoked as patron and prophet of healthier and more attractive modes of modernity", including scientific inquiry and
religious critique (*Victorians*, 84). The question, it seemed, was the extent of
Lucretius's rationalism and the significance of his passion. Put another way, was
De Rerum Natura a philosophical exposition of Epicureanism or a poetic revelation of personality? Tennyson's "Lucretius" intervenes in this question and
recasts it in terms of the quest for transcendence. Redirecting the significance
of Lucretius from scientific rationalism to the good life and using Jerome's story
as a very particular ending of a life, the poem implicitly argues that the rationalistic, positivistic aspects of Lucretius, when turned into ethical or moral principles, become entirely hostile to the good life.

*

    In the poem, Tennyson's Lucretius enacts his self-ignorance, self-
awareness, and self-annihilation through an unearthing of his repressed sexual
desires. The frame of the poem indicates his lack of warmth towards his wife and
suggests that he has buried his physical lusts. He has formed an erotic relation
to Epicurus, pursuing the latter's path and longing for god-like tranquility. As
the poem progresses and Lucretius's sanity ebbs, he is increasingly forced to
acknowledge his own sexual desires. These desires are not toward any particular
object (his wife or Epicurus, for example) but are rather more like energies of
his body or facts of his (sub)consciousness. His denial of these lusts brings on
insanity, and only with his eventual recognition of them does he regain clarity
and, ironically, the self-resolve necessary to kill himself.
    Lucretius's intention throughout his monologue is to compose himself
after a night of terrible dreams, that is, to regain tranquility. This intention

---

14 This dynamic takes its most pure form in a poem like Hölderlin's "Hyperions
    Schicksalslied" ("Hyperion's Song of Fate"), but is also recognizable in more
    complicated ways in poems such as Coleridge's *Rime of the Ancient Mariner*,
    Shelley's *Mont Blanc*, and Keats's "Bright star! would I were steadfast as thou art".
    It is also found in Nietzsche's understanding of the Apollonian and Dionysian in *The
    Birth of Tragedy* (1872), which was first published within four years of "Lucretius".

---

illuminates his sexual desires and makes it ever more clear that he is unable to master them.[15] In the recounting of his dreams, we see that, on some level, he sees himself as a masculine figure battling feminine passions, a self-image that is in tension with his longing for transcendence. It is debatable at what point he first (dimly) intends suicide, yet it is clear that this act becomes a way to unite the figure of masculine warrior with the seeker of transcendence and tranquility. Tennyson, through his attention to Lucretius's complicated thinking, makes him a sympathetic figure whose devotion to the Epicurean ideal becomes a denial of human life: His attempt at self-composure becomes an act of self-annihilation.

Lucretius's first words, "Storm in the night", are, as Linda Hughes points out, an "emblem of his own mind" (*Manyfacèd*, 226). The tempest without is mirrored by the storm within. He begins with the three dreams of the previous night, two of which are sexually charged and suggest subconscious desires and lusts. Tennyson's Lucretius alludes to the theory of dreams found in *De Rerum Natura*, "that the mind is occupied in sleep by whatever employment has the greatest hold on one's interest, or by whatever one did in his last waking hours" (4.962–1036), but these dreams obviously demand a more Freudian analysis (Markley, *Stateliest*, 142). While he is able to claim the first dream as his own, that is, as originating in his daily preoccupations (Tennyson, "Lucretius", 43–46), the second dream surprises him:

> I thought that all the blood by Sylla shed
> Came driving down again on earth,
> And where it dashed the reddening meadow, sprang
> No dragon warriors from Cadmean teeth,
> For these I thought my dream would show to me,

---

15 In formulating this dynamic, I draw on Cornelia D. J. Pearsall's discussion of Tennyson's achievement in the dramatic monologue and her use of J. L. Austin's notion of intention. According to Pearsall, the "dominant critical claim" about Victorian dramatic monologues is that "speakers [...] reveal themselves in unwitting ways in the course of the monologue, so that the revelations that occur are considered unconscious or accidental, thus wholly subverting any discernable discursive intentions" (Pearsall, *Tennyson's Rapture*, 24). Pearsall suggests a more subtle dynamic by introducing J. L. Austin's rather poetic description of intention as "a miner's lamp on our forehead which illuminates always just so far ahead as we go along. [...] The only general rule is that the illumination is always *limited*, and that in several ways. It will never extend indefinitely far ahead" (Pearsall, *Tennyson's Rapture*, 24; Austin, *Papers*, 284). In introducing this richer idea of intention to her study of the dramatic monologue, Pearsall is able to theorize and describe a more subtle psychology at work in the dramatic monologue. Austin's imagery is particularly appropriate for "Lucretius" because, as I've suggested above, the poetry is unearthing passions that have been buried in an attempt to achieve tranquility.

But girls, Hetairai, curious in their art,
Hired animalisms, vile as those that made
The mulberry-faced Dictator's orgies worse
Than aught they fable of the quiet Gods.
And hands they mixt, and yelled and round me drove
In narrowing circles till I yelled again
Half-suffocated, and sprang up, and saw—
Was it the first beam of my latest day? (Tennyson, "Lucretius", 47–59)

The dream views the recent dictatorship of Sulla in 81 BC (when the historical Lucretius would have been in his late teens) in terms of the mythological tale of Cadmus sowing the dragon's teeth. The dictator's massacres, a mythic allegory might suggest, would give rise to republican, armed resistance. Despite the surreal quality, this overlay of recent history and myth suggests a controlled, political allegory. But sexuality disrupts things. In stating what he "thought [his] dream would show [him]", Lucretius admits his surprise as the phallic "dragon warriors" are supplanted by the vampiric Hetairai that surround and close in on him until he wakes in terror.

Though there is surely much to be said about this dream, I merely wish to point out that this passage suggests the return of the repressed. Despite Lucretius's belief that dreams rehearse daily concerns, this dream clearly shows Lucretius something about himself that he does not recognize. In particular, martial masculinity is supplanted by sexualized femininity. His dream reveals that he sees himself as a militant defender of the Epicurean way, losing the battle with his own desires.

If this dream shows the battle symbolically through the appearance of women rather than the expected warriors, then the final dream is much more explicit in staging the confrontation between masculine virtue and feminine eroticism.[16] Lucretius's third and final dream, which involves the breasts of Helen and a sword, alludes to the story of Menelaus's confrontation with Helen when the Greeks finally took Troy. At this point, the Greeks have been at war with Troy for ten years, all in an attempt to reclaim Helen from Paris. Menelaus, no longer concerned with salvaging his marriage, is ready to kill this cursed woman who has caused so much suffering. Despite the obvious sexism of his intention, such vengeance can be read as a virtuous act of justice. Yet, Helen shows her breast, and Menelaus's resolve fails. Just so, in Lucretius's dream, the sword

Pointed itself to pierce, but sank down shamed
At all that beauty. (Tennyson, 63–64)

---

16 For a compelling reading of this dream, on which I draw, see Freeman's "'Lucretius' and the 'Breasts of Helen'".

The image is obviously one of impotence. Upon waking and thereby escaping the Heterai, Lucretius "sprang up", but within five lines the sword "sank down" (58, 63). Again, erotic femininity defeats martial masculinity.

But of course the eroticism is not Lucretius's external enemy but a part of himself that he has suppressed in order to follow Epicurus's path. There is something delusional in figuring the struggle with desire—which is actually a desire for transcendence—in these heroic terms, and so the climax of this psychological drama begins with a figure not of heroic struggle but of a nostalgic yearning for transcendence that is counterpointed with bodily, animal lust. Lucretius contemplates the landscape, the mountain that has weathered the night's storm and has returned to serenity, and wonders why he cannot, like Nature, "smile / [...] / At random ravage" (Tennyson, 174–176). His stream of thought is associative, and this combination of knowledge about nature and confusion about self leads him to recall the story of Numa, who by capturing Picus and Faunus, learned how to avert Jove's lightning.[17] As Markley writes, the story "demonstrates a mythological account of humans' successful acquisition of information about the gods" that is suggestive of Lucretius's scientific project (*Stateliest*, 144). However, as in the dream involving the Cadmus myth, Lucretius is unable to limit the significance of the myth and the allegorized tale becomes a "pastoral hallucination" (*Stateliest*, 144). The allegory of scientific pursuit devolves to a fantasy of erotic pursuit:

> And here an Oread—how the sun delights
> To glance and shift about her slippery sides,
> And rosy knees and supple roundedness,
> And budded bosom-peaks—who this way runs
> Before the rest—A satyr, a satyr, see,
> Follows. (Tennyson, 188–193)

The lines that follow suggest confusion and even madness. Lucretius literally "sees" this chase, though he tells himself that he has proved satyrs impossible. Thus, his disbelief unwillingly suspended, he looks at the satyr with disgust, identifying with the nymph who "loathes him as well". But he then asks, "will she fling herself, / Shamelessly upon me?" and now identifying with the satyr, he urges, "Catch her, goat-foot" (200–202). Aware above all of his own confusion, the vision ends with the following lines:

>   nay,
> Hide, hide them, million-myrtled wilderness,
> And cavern-shadowing laurels, hide! do I wish—
> What?—that the bushes were leafless? or to whelm
> All in one massacre? (Tennyson, 203–207)

---

17 See Ricks' note at Tennyson, "Lucretius", 181–182.

Finally, at this moment, the self-denial that would hide desire is relinquished and the wish to bare all, even to extinguish all, is admitted—or at least entertained as a possibility.

Quite unexpectedly, then, the quasi-scientific observation of nature that would facilitate self-control and unlock the secrets of the so-called gods is turned into a phantasmagoric, multi-faceted mirror in which Lucretius sees his desires and wishes. And with this vision comes a moment of lucidity, apparently brought on by the articulation of the hitherto unspoken; the disjointed and erratic syntax relaxes into a calm and considered apostrophe to the gods in which he confesses his ambition and failure to live carelessly and serenely as they:

> O ye Gods,
> I know you careless, yet, behold, to you
> From childly wont and ancient use I call—
> I thought I lived securely as yourselves—
> No lewdness, narrowing envy, monkey-spite,
> No madness of ambition, avarice, none;
>
> . . . .
>
> But now it seems some unseen monster lays
> His vast and filthy hands upon my will. (Tennyson, 207–20)

The possibility that the human could become godlike is given up, and Lucretius prays. Even while holding onto his belief that the gods are not interested in human affairs, he prays, "From childly wont and ancient use." The self-humbling is poignant and pathetic, and though firmly rooted in the fiction of the poem, Tennyson with it suggests to his contemporaries the continuing relevance of belief, not just as an emotional comfort but as a way to cope and perhaps come to terms with the brutal (brutish?) reality of the human condition.[18]

Christianity, of course, has historically acknowledged these human realities but consigned them to sinful human nature. Lucretius's description of the "unseen monster" with its "vast and filthy hands upon my will" reads like an archaic attempt to understand sin, and it reminds me of God's words to Cain before he murders Abel, in particular his warning that "at the tent flap sin crouches / And for you is its longing" (Genesis 4:7, trans. Alter). Lucretius is far more self-aware than Cain, especially at this point of the poem; still, like Cain he responds with violence.

Lucretius rouses himself to suicide by claiming it as the "privilege" of a

---

18 Compare Lucretius's alienation from the gods and his resulting prayer with Tennyson's pronouncements at the dinner with Symonds: "The human soul seems to me always in some way, how we do not know, identical with God. That's the value of prayer. Prayer is like opening a sluice between the great ocean and our little channels" (Symonds, *Letters*, 6).

---

man, indeed of a Roman. Through a series of rhetorical questions he recalls the imagery of a masculine virtue that will overcome beastlike desires. One question, in particular, draws my attention:

> And what man
> What Roman would be dragged in triumph thus?
> (Tennyson, 233–234)

In using the image of a triumph, Tennyson suggests his hero is aware that his defeat from (internal) passions resembles defeat from (external) enemies. In both cases, the possibility of tranquility is disrupted by that which is beyond the individual's control.[19]

By the end of his poem, we can see that, through the use of Jerome's story, Tennyson has turned Lucretius's philosophy into a kind of ironic tragedy. Epicurus had claimed to have "gotten ahead" of *Tuchē*, which is exactly the kind of transcendence that Lucretius sought, but he has remained vulnerable to chance, as we all do. Ironically, the acceptance of nature that Lucretius seems to advocate could have reconciled him to his own desires, yet his insistence on godlike tranquility precluded such acceptance. The claim by one critic that, by having Lucretius suffer from the love philter, Tennyson tests his philosophy "in adversity" (Hughes, *Manyfacèd*, 231), misstates the case by adopting the same heroic ethos that Lucretius seems to want in his imagery of warriors. Tennyson's more basic point is that human life is subject to chance. On the one hand, that may mean the jealousy of a wife and the unforeseen consequences of her actions; on the other hand it may mean madness and suicide. "Lucretius" shows the futile attempts to fight this truth about the human condition. Strangely, what might seem a heroic tragedy turns darkly ironic given the way Lucretius's devotion to the godlike ideal of Epicureanism works against him.

Tennyson's reflection on the ideal of tranquility, then, turns out to be extraordinarily sensitive and nuanced—surprisingly so, if we consider Symonds's short sketch of the poet. Later, when Symonds read the published poem, he

---

19 It is also significant that the Roman Lucretius envisions himself as a victim of a (presumably) Roman triumph, which reminds us that Lucretius lived near the end of the Roman Republic, when civil wars created the possibility that a Roman would drag another Roman in triumph. Ironically, before killing himself Lucretius recalls the story of Lucrece, from whose suicide "sprang the Commonwealth [i.e., the Republic], which breaks / As I am breaking now!" (Tennyson, 241–242). See Pearsall, who quotes these lines and asserts: "Every major Tennysonian dramatic monologist similarly recognizes, as did the poet, the profound homology between his own transformations, willing or unwilling, and those of the society to which he is so intimately bound or from which he is rapturously borne away" (Pearsall, *Tennyson's Rapture*, 13).

---

declared it "perhaps the most splendid of all Tennyson's essays in blank-verse, and the most gorgeously coloured piece of unrhymed English since Milton", yet he did not like it. "Its action is slow and rotatory", he complained, "not swift, simple, straightforward, like tiger-leaps or lightning-flashes, as it ought to be" (Symonds, *Letters*, 20). If the characterization is accurate, the judgment is unfair. The achievement is precisely in the careful representation not of concluded thought but of stumbling and slow thinking, which is to say the "profound moral earnestness" that Symonds had earlier admired in Tennyson. The anxieties that Tennyson had revealed to the young critic were personal and national, provincial and prejudiced, and apparently unexplored. The poem, however, concerned with the modern and engaged with the ancient, a revelation of personality through philosophical reflection, displays not only Lucretius's futility but Tennyson's insight.

SELECT BIBLIOGRAPHY

Allen, Katherine. "Lucretius the Poet and Tennyson's Poem 'Lucretius'". *Poet-Lore* 9 (1899): 529–548.

Alter, Robert, trans. *Genesis: Translation and Commentary.* New York: Norton, 1996.

Austin, J. L. *Philosophical Papers.* 2nd ed. Edited by J. O. Urmson and G. J. Warnock. Oxford: Clarendon, 1970.

Chesterton, G. K. *The Victorian Age in Literature.* New York: Holt, 1913.

Freeman, James A. "'Lucretius' and the 'Breasts of Helen'". *Victorian Poetry* 11, no. 1 (1973): 69–75.

Jebb, R. C. "On Mr. Tennyson's 'Lucretius'". *Macmillan's Magazine* 18 (1868): 97–103.

Hölderlin, Friedrich. "Hyperion's Song of Fate". In *German Poetry from 1750–1900*, edited by Robert M. Browning, 90–93. Translated by Christopher Middleton. New York: Continuum, 1984.

Hughes, Linda K. *The Manyfacèd Glass: Tennyson's Dramatic Monologues.* Athens, Ohio: Ohio University Press, 1987.

Locke, John. *An Essay Concerning Human Understanding.* Edited by Peter H. Nidditch. Oxford: Clarendon, 1975.

Lucretius. *De Rerum Natura*. Translated by W. H. D. Rouse. Revised by Martin Ferguson Smith. Cambridge, Mass.: Harvard University Press, Loeb Classical Library, 1992.

Markley, A. A. *Stateliest Measures: Tennyson and the Literature of Greece and Rome*. Toronto: University of Toronto Press, 2004.

Mustard, Wilfred. "Tennyon and Lucretius". In *Classical Echoes in Tennyson*, by Mustard. London: Macmillan, 1904.

Nietzsche, Friedrich. *The Birth of Tragedy and Other Writings*. Edited by Raymond Geuss and Ronald Speirs. Translated by Ronald Speirs. Cambridge: Cambridge University Press, 1999.

Nussbaum, Martha C. *The Fragility of Goodness: Luck and Ethics in Greek Tragedy and Philosophy*. Cambridge: Cambridge University Press, 1986.

———. *The Therapy of Desire: Theory and Practice in Hellenistic Ethics*. Princeton: Princeton University Press, 1994.

Pearsall, Cornelia D. J. *Tennyson's Rapture: Transformation in the Victorian Dramatic Monologue*. New York: Oxford University Press, 2008.

Ricks, Christopher. *Tennyson*. New York: Macmillan, 1972.

Symonds, John Addington. *Letters and Papers of John Addington Symonds*. Edited by Horatio F. Brown. London: John Murray, 1923.

Tennyson, Alfred. "Lucretius". In *The Poems of Tennyson*, edited by Christopher Ricks, 1206–1207. Harlow: Longmans, 1969.

Vance, Norman. *The Victorians and Ancient Rome*. Oxford: Blackwell, 1997.

Wilner, Ortha. "Tennyson and Lucretius". *Classical Journal* 25 (1930): 347–366.

HOW EPICUREAN SCIENCE SAVES HUMANITY
IN LUCRETIUS

John R. Lenz

INTRODUCTION: SCIENCE AND HUMANITIES TOGETHER AGAIN

Ancient Greek philosophy teaches that knowledge provides humans both happiness and salvation. Ancient philosophy isn't usually taught that way: *philosophy saves!* But before psychology, before psychotherapy, there was *philosophy*. Philosophy was therapy for human souls; "soul" meant our entire inner life; and the best part of our soul is our rational mind.

How does knowledge save us? By offering a vision of a life after death? Yes, for some ancient Greeks, most notably Plato, salvation was metaphysical: You had to be dead to get it.[1] For Epicureans such as Lucretius, an afterlife is neither possible nor necessary; we can attain bliss while alive by developing our mind. Philosophy, not religion,[2] is the only way to attain the elevated life of a god while we are alive.

What kind of knowledge? Knowledge of everything: of the way the world works, and in particular, knowledge of the hidden causes of all things. Lucretius's poem *De Rerum Natura* explains physics (the workings of *phusis*, nature), psychology, epistemology, religion, myth, meteorology, and more. All this has implications for the human soul. Ancient thought did not separate science and humanities.

"By nature all men desire to know", said Aristotle.[3] "Science" (a Latin word) means "knowledge". Human beings, for the Greeks, are part of the natural world (*phusis*) and to understand ourselves, we must understand nature (*phusiologia*). Indeed, understanding the universe (the *cosmos*) is necessary for realizing our cosmic origin, role and purpose, if any. While different ancient schools held different views on this, the "big picture" idea of human beings as part of the *cosmos* seems to be a still-useful feature of ancient thought (despite atavistic misuses such as astrology).[4] True, the implications of this perspective

---

1   Plato's Socrates says the goal of philosophy is to prepare us to die (*Phaedo* 64a). After death, the philosopher enjoys blissful visions (*Phaedrus*, *Republic*); "and it will save us too", says Socrates (*Rep.* 621c1) of the Myth of Er whose cosmic vision concludes the *Republic*.

2   As Charles Natoli shows in this volume, all religion is superstition for Lucretius.

3   Aristotle, *Metaphysics* 980a1 (the first sentence of the work).

4   Brague, *The Wisdom of the World*, and (from a Christian perspective) Martin, *Inventing Superstition*. Complete bibliographic information for all non-Classical works cited can be found in the Select Bibliography at the end of this essay.

---

can be taken in different ways. Traditional humanism often magnifies human beings to the center of attention (thus *e.g.* animals do not have immortal souls in Christianity), while for others a cosmic perspective diminishes humans by reducing them to insignificant ephemeral specks. The phrase "human nature" suggests an essential link between science and humanities, even though the concept of "nature" and its applicability to human society remain much contested.

In today's academic world, science and humanities usually inhabit separate worlds, famously called the "two cultures".[5] In the United States at present, creationists oppose, and humanities students and teachers reject, science ("I'm not a science type"). What is lost? Science becomes technology, the human mind does not see all it can, and uncritical religious attitudes persist. This paper will defend the benefit of Lucretius as a possible antidote today. Ironically, Catherine Wilson suggests that it was the very success of Epicurean-type scientific materiality that led, in early modern times, to the split between natural science and other disciplines such as ethics and metaphysics;[6] that is to say, other, not empirically objective ways of understanding our place in the universe. However, one could also say that this split causes writers on Lucretius and Epicureanism in the history of science[7] to ignore the place of the scientific world-view in the full Epicurean system of ethics and human happiness.

One reason for the common supposed divide between science and the humanities, today and historically, is to defend and protect the sphere of religion. Thomas Aquinas provides a canonical yet shocking formulation of this. He argued for two irreconcilable types of knowledge, science and faith. He said that reason studies the things of this world (this represents his compromise with contemporary "Aristotelianism"), but revelation and faith are required for salvation. Reason does not apply to that realm, he says explicitly, because reason cannot demonstrate or even defend what is believed by faith:

> Hence that the world began to exist is an object of faith, but not of demonstration or science. And it is useful to consider this, lest anyone, presuming to demonstrate what is of faith, should bring forward reasons that are not cogent, so as to give occasion to unbelievers to laugh, thinking that on such grounds we believe things that are of faith. [*Summa Theologica* 1a.46.2]

This refusal to rationally discuss the objects of faith pertaining to religion—which does after all make large claims about the world—is all too

---

5   C. P. Snow's 1959 formulation has generated much debate; *e.g.* Barash, "C. P. Snow".

6   Wilson, *Epicureanism*, vi.

7   Johnson and Wilson, "Lucretius and the History of Science"; Wilson, *Epicureanism*.

common today, with harmful consequences.[8] Like modern hardliners W. K. Clifford and Bertrand Russell, Lucretius says nothing good can come of wrong ideas or ideas unsupported by reason. He shares the view of a number of ancient Greek philosophers that our only salvation lies in reason.

A second mainstay of the contemporary gulf between science and humanities is the "fact/value" distinction. We often hear that science gives us facts but not values. For example: science can tell us how to build a bomb, but not whether to use it. In fact, science has been under a cloud—a mushroom cloud—of suspicion for a long time. But the fact/value distinction is not always a good one. Cannot values be based on truths? To put it another way, Lucretius is often admired for being both an artist and a natural philosopher. Many readers, and too many scholars, find this combination paradoxical; but the two are inseparable in his work, where good science entails the best humanity and vice versa.[9]

A third way to describe the "split" is that humanists shelter their sphere—the human soul ("know yourself")—from the practical arts of manipulating matter. Historically, humanism has often been imbued with spiritual qualities. With Socrates as a foundational ancestor (*e.g.* Plato, *Phaedo* 96a-99c), thinkers from Mary Shelley ("the modern Prometheus") to Heidegger and Marcuse warn about the dangers of science working against humanity ("technological man"). On the other side, some, such as John Locke and John Dewey, advocate a practical, "hands-on", experimental education. Lucretius does not share that pragmatic view of science. Indeed he praises but also warns about technology. He does not think all progress is good. Once a comfortable civilization has been achieved (summarized at 5.1448-1457), more things do not bring more happiness for people. People increase their desires, they want more, they fight wars over things, and nothing is ever enough. People need to manage *themselves*. To serve that purpose, he presents a broader view of science as complete knowledge of the natural world and our place in it. Whatever we think of the pluses and minuses of technology, we must not forget the value of this meaning of science as understanding for thinking humanity.

An even worse (fourth) threat today is the axiom that culture trumps nature; that the humanities are entirely governed by, and consist largely of, politics, where politics involves defining one's identity by relation to various groups. Epicurus, like most ancient Greek philosophers, believed that wisdom was outside of and above politics, in understanding the universe and ourselves, together. Talk by scholars of Lucretius's own politics, his Roman context and his use of political imagery, is of course useful and interesting, but diverts attention from the cosmic and human wisdom. Rational knowledge, accessible to all

---

8   See Harris, *The End of Faith.*

9   Johnson, *Lucretius*, chapter 5 provides a fascinating discussion of the usefulness of Lucretius for a contemporary scientific ethic. However what I mean here is more than the ethics of doing and using science well.

---

human beings through our minds, provides the best means of living well, as we shall see. This is not the popular Aristotelian practical wisdom.

On these general points, Lucretius may still provide some guidance. People need science (in this broad sense) to achieve human wisdom, full humanity, and happiness. Epicurus, Lucretius's master, himself hated purely literary culture. It is not that he disliked poetry and art. Rather, *paideia* enshrined conventional culture with its myths and superstitions (much like Plato's criticism of poetry). Text- and word- (*logos-*) based humanities often preserve a somewhat religious notion of a human-centered universe and certain traditional spiritual ideals. Without science, humanists are "professors of rhetoric".[10] However, Lucretius answers Epicurus's criticism (and even Plato's) by combining poetry with a new science and accompanying new spiritual ideals.

LUCRETIUS'S SCIENCE: SOME GENERAL POINTS

We may define science philosophically as rational contemplation of ultimate truths, in particular, the causes of things, the sources of birth and death, (in Greek terms) the eternal Being behind the processes of Becoming. The ultimate truths for Lucretius and Epicureans are in a word: atoms. Knowledge of atoms and their operation, that is of physical processes that govern everything in the universe without exception, will (we shall see) free our minds and light the way to the truest happiness.

The *De Rerum Natura* of Lucretius helps us to heal an artificial divide between science and humanities. Not because he is equally skillful at poetry and natural philosophy both. To draw attention to that (as Santayana does, for example), is to preserve the idea that the two do not ordinarily go together. Some say that Lucretius is a good poet but a bad scientist. I disagree. Although some have thought him an "embarrassing ancestor" of modern science, Lucretius can still be considered a precursor of modern scientific or Enlightenment thought; his account of evolution can be compared with Darwin's.[11] But rather than discuss scientific points, I'd like to look at the big picture, his rational method and the virtue of scientific contemplation or *theoria* for the humanities. Lucretius is a good humanist because he is a good scientific thinker.

In announcing his task, Lucretius states that science has the goal of freeing the mind:

---

10 Johnson, *Lucretius*, 80; generally, Asmis, "Epicurean Poetics".

11 Johnson, *Lucretius*, 89 (quoted) and 94; Campbell, *Lucretius* on 5.772–1104; see the note on Spinoza, below. For Lucretius's reputation and influence, see, besides those works, Johnson and Wilson, "Lucretius and the History of Science", Jones, *The Epicurean Tradition,* Turner, "Lucretius among the Victorians", and Wilson, *Epicureanism.*

This terrifying darkness that enshrouds the mind must be dispelled not by the sun's rays [...] but by study of the superficial aspect and underlying principle of nature. [1.146–148][12]

He is interested in science not for its own sake, but for our own ultimate good. (Epicurus himself lacked interest in some branches of science, such as astronomy.[13]) Science serves ethics, psychology, and peace of mind: in short, human happiness.

Science means not technology, not the practical manipulation of matter, but knowledge of the physical world, of nature and nature's laws. Of course his method is empirical. We can only know through our senses. But the visible leads to the invisible; through reasoning and the use of analogy, clues lead to underlying causes.

The method is the important thing, even when he is wrong or uncertain. He attempts to provide possible explanations of things we do not have good close experience of, such as the formation of lightning through collisions in clouds (6.96-422) without recourse to gods. When you remember that the philosopher Anaxagoras was run out of 5th century BCE Athens for positing that the sun and moon were bodies and not gods, you can see how sophisticated Lucretius was in explaining all phenomena without positing superhuman or supernatural divine agency. (Pierre Bayle was similarly ahead of his time in the 1682 debate on comets.)

At times he admirably suggests multiple possible causes in order to keep alternatives open (6.703–711). This is basic scientific method, to be careful to say when he does not know:

Which of these causes operates in our world it is difficult to determine with certainty. [...] I am striving to set out several causes that may account for the motions of the stars [...]. [T]o assert dogmatically which of them it is, certainly does not befit one proceeding with cautious steps. [5.526–533]

The ultimate causes are atoms, all atoms; nothing but atoms, their types (shape, size, weight) and motions. Epicureanism presents just about the most extreme materialism ever (earning for this many enemies). Everything is made of atoms, even the soul. There is no separate type of thing called a soul. This demolishes idealistic dualism. Mind (although harder to explain) does not exist outside and apart from the body and the workings of atoms. This poses a challenge to traditional humanism with its often spiritual aura.

---

12 All quotations from *De Rerum Natura* are from the 2001 Smith prose translation unless otherwise noted.

13 Courtney, "Epicurus", 254; Smith, *Lucretius*, 2001, 151n38.

Gods are not needed to explain the process of the creation of natural bodies. The gods themselves are made of atoms and play no part in our world. Atoms are eternal and imperishable. Our world was not made by a creator out of nothing. Can something be created out of nothing? A "no" answer leans to atheism.[14]

The collisions of atoms cause bodies to be formed. Atoms move at uniform speeds but are subject to that pesky "swerve" just to make things unpredictable. Still, chance does *not* rule our world (Long, "Chance and Laws of Nature in Epicureanism"). Our world is governed by orderly natural law— for example, species have certain properties and animals can only mate with members of the same species—and Lucretius's task is to explain that rational order: "by what law each thing has its scope restricted and its deeply implanted boundary stone" (1.76–77).

The world is materialistic, but materialism is not the end of the story. Epicurus and Lucretius are materialists but not determinists. The unpredictability of atomic swerve (a knotty concept) is meant to avoid determinism. Besides that they are modified materialists in another more important but less discussed way. They are not ethical materialists. The goal of the system is not material but ethical; a theory of atoms leads to the best *human* values. The humanistic rewards of Epicurean scientific theory will be set out in the next two sections, leading to the suggestion that Epicureanism does put mind above matter.

Epicurean science in Lucretius explains more than our world containing our earth. The entire universe is infinite and contains infinite worlds (2.1048ff). Our world is imperfect and will perish. In a blow to the "argument from design", the argument that the world is so perfect it must have a creator, Lucretius notes that the world evinces poor design at best, being "marked by such serious flaws" (5.199). The world was not made for people (5.156ff), and humans are not at the center. This has surprisingly positive implications for ethics. As Brague points out, it is no longer possible for humans to imitate or assimilate themselves to the world-order, as other ethical systems enjoin (Plato and the Stoics).[15] Paradoxically, because our lives do not have a goal (there is no cosmic teleology), the goal becomes understanding this state of affairs through the mind. Epicureanism rescues us from becoming depressed in realizing we are only "specks" in the scheme of things; partly we are and partly we are not. Our bodies and short lives are. Humans are part of nature (made by the natural processes of atoms). Our minds (I shall argue) are and are not (being not fully subject to necessity). Here we benefit from the non-deterministic loophole in atomism. Epicurean science teaches not only a cosmic science, but a meta-

---

14 A defining feature of Enlightenment "Spinozism" was the radically threatening view that motion is present in matter. Similarly Lucretius' idea of mind, while not able to be fully explained materially, is naturalistic.

15 Brague, *Wisdom*, 41: "The final arrangement is not order [...] but atoms and the void."

cosmic perspective,[16] as we confront the fact of death and rise above it through having reached in our minds a perspective on the whole.

KNOWLEDGE ABOUT DEATH: HOMER'S ODYSSEUS AS OPPOSED TO LUCRETIUS

The ultimate knowledge is knowledge of the causes of birth and death: a cosmological, existential vision. Epicurus, Lucretius says, has uncovered this hidden truth (e.g. 3.14-40). Likewise, the "mystery of his birth" impels Oedipus's search as told by Sophocles.[17] He learned that his birth was given him by the gods and not by chance. *The Epic of Gilgamesh* begins,

He saw the Secret, discovered the Hidden, /
he brought information of (the time) before the Flood.
(*Gilgamesh*, 1.5–6)

Specifically, Gilgamesh learns that all human beings must die. Oedipus and Gilgamesh both end up as wise men due to their existential knowledge.

The stakes of science for Lucretius are nothing less than that kind of ultimate knowledge. His poem begins with birth and ends with death (Clay, "Sources", 19).

Epicureanism teaches us to be mortal. Being mortal, we can learn to be happy. This is better than striving after a vain hope of immortality. In fact, knowing that we die is precisely the first key to becoming happy. Epicureanism reaches the knowledge of mortality in an interesting way as compared with other types of accounts which typically reside in the genre of myth-historical literature.

In Homer's *Odyssey*, Odysseus visits the shades of the dead. He sees the ghost of his mother, who explains to him what death is like, so that, she adjures, he may know this and tell another when he returns to the living (11.216–224). Achilles tells him (11.488–491) that it is better to be virtually the lowliest man on earth than king of the dead. Thus knowledge of death—there is no salvation—provides a lesson on how to live (*carpe diem*, said Horace).

Myth works this way. We have a story (*muthos*), a fiction, of a hero, Odysseus, who went "where no man had gone before" and returned with the story to educate mortals about death and give advice on how to live. In fact, Odysseus's voyage to encounter the dead probably owes something to the earlier story of Gilgamesh (mentioned above). Homer's poems provided powerful, perhaps formative teachings for subsequent Greek culture,[18] just as today another

---

16 Brague, *Wisdom*, 43 calls it "non-cosmic".

17 Sophocles, *Oedipus the King*, line 1059: "Fail to solve the mystery of my birth (*genos*)?" The seer Tiresias predicts the consequences of knowledge (line 438): "This day will bring your birth and your destruction." (trans. R. Fagles)

18 Herodotus said that Homer and Hesiod taught the Greeks about the gods (*Histories* 2. 53).

John R. Lenz

ancient book (really a collection of books), the Bible (the second part of which is written in ancient Greek), still does for major world religions. God is a literary character in this work. Modern notions of Hell owe something to a literary-artistic tradition that includes Dante's poem *Inferno* (c. 1300).

The Australian philosopher David Stove[19] calls this the Ishmael strategy in epistemology: we are asked to take the word of one person who has seen something special. Religions often work that way. The Gospels report what a few people supposedly saw, the resurrected Jesus; if an author asserts the existence of more witnesses, this still means that in practice we have there one witness. Even so, it is fascinating, and not sufficiently noticed, how religions acknowledge that they do need some empirical evidence. As a religion originating in history, Christianity claims to be based on actual verifiable facts or events. Major religions of the world are based on ancient stories.

Compare Homer's Odysseus with Lucretius, who is also writing a literary work in ancient times, but based on reason. Odysseus's experience was bodily (he went there), empirical (for him but for no one else), and presented in literary fiction. The valuable lesson he conveys dwells on the misery of death in the absence of the body. Lucretius too makes a descent into the realm of death, but with reasoned theory. He makes a philosophical *katabasis* (descent) in order to rise above death. He uses a theoretical science of atoms—a theory of invisible causes—to teach about bodies, their formation and decay. However, his real goal does not concern bodies, but the human mind (we will discuss this more). Nothing is exempt from reason. The poet does not claim privileged access to something only he knows. He must persuade us. All human beings can have access to ultimate knowledge, and its rewards. While the goal is a high one that some might find to be elitist (on the lines of the well-known criticism of Plato)—having attained the highest knowledge and peace, the philosopher sits atop a hierarchy of less-valued behaviors and less well-behaved values stemming from the passions—this goal is potentially open democratically to all human beings.

One objection must be met. Lucretius and Epicurus do not tell us to do science ourselves. They give us overarching ultimate conclusions reached through reasoning, not experiment. We hear Lucretius expound the system; and Epicureanism was renowned for not changing much in the centuries after the founder. Does this come to us as revelation? Are we to take the conclusions as dogma? No. Lucretius's task is to persuade us through reason. If our reason assents to his arguments, we thus engage in the acquisition of knowledge. For this reason, *De Rerum Natura* is full of more detailed arguments than many readers might expect or want. Some scholars of literature hold that Lucretius sways us with his powerful image-rich verse. Of course. But however tremendous the poetry, it is a means to an end; awesome as the poetry is, we should not think that his poetic devices serve to manipulate the readers' emotions *against* reason.

---

19 Stove, "'I only am escaped alone […]'".

Today, many hold that reason is elitist. (The privileging of reason, in one way or another, is typical of most ancient Greek philosophy.) Yet it is potentially democratic, something within all human beings. Everyone can see for themselves. You don't have to visit Hades. It's not enough to believe what you read in the *Odyssey* or in the Old or New Testaments, or to take an Epicurus on faith. Lucretius asks you to travel to the limits of the universe, using your own mind to see (if you assent) the truth that is the same for all human beings.

EPICUREAN PHILOSOPHY SAVES: (I) LIVING WELL

Lucretius depicts Epicurus as a godlike savior for the ills plaguing mankind. We must take seriously the notion of philosophy as therapeutic and in some sense salvific. Working through the Epicurean system is not like taking a Philosophy class today. It is not like doing analytical philosophy, although it makes use of rigorous logical tools. Thus, it confounds the current Analytical/ Continental divide, as does most ancient philosophy. Remember, Plato concluded the *Republic* with the Myth of Er, who had been brought back from death to describe the afterlife and the workings of the universe;[20] Socrates asserts that this story "will save us too" (621c1).

Epicurus wrote: "Vain is the word of a philosopher by whom no human suffering is cured. [....] [P]hilosophy is of no use if it fails to banish the suffering of the mind."[21] His second-century-AD follower Diogenes of Oenoanda spoke, in words inscribed on walls for public benefit, of "the medications which bring salvation".[22] Lucretius sees himself as a missionary.[23]

Epicureanism subordinates science to ethics. Good science leads to better ethics and a better life. The reward of knowledge comes not from practical applications of technology to the world of matter—values are not found in matter—but in the mental realm itself. The best human life is lived with a state of mind acquired through knowledge.

Philosophy, in particular the Epicurean scientific system of knowledge of the world, saves us (our inner selves) in two ways. One is more practical (and results from ridding us of "negative" beliefs); the other (more controversial) is contemplative and a "positive" good in itself.[24]

---

20 Of relevance in reading Lucretius, as developed below in this paper, is that Er observed from without, in an act of *theoria,* the Spindle of Necessity. His own observing (contemplative) mind is at that moment outside of necessity. I thank Vishwa Adluri for showing me this.

21 Epicurus fr. 221 (Usener); quoted from Smith, *Lucretius,* 2001, xxiii.

22 "ta tes soterias protheinai pharmaka", quoted from Clay, *Paradosis,* 201.

23 Smith, *Lucretius,* 1992, xxvi, and Smith, *Lucretius,* 2001, xxxiii.

24 Similarly, Epicurus describes two types of happiness: one which can be added to or subtracted from, and "the highest possible, such as the gods enjoy" (Diog. Laert. 10.121).

Lucretius offers practical, real-life benefits: acquiring the scientific knowledge he preaches leads to a better life. For example:

"you are learning to understand the whole nature of things and perceive its utility [*utilitas*]" (4.24–25);

Epicurus "discovered that reasoned plan of life [*vitae rationem*] which is now called wisdom [*sapientia*]" (5.9–10);

"good life [*bene ... vivi*] was impossible without a purged mind" (5.18–19);

and from these teachings "come sweet consolations of life [*dulcia ... solacia vitae*] to soothe our minds" (5.21).[25]

Epicurus himself stresses the necessity of knowledge: "It was impossible for someone ignorant about the nature of the universe [...] to dissolve his feelings of fear about the most important matters. So it was impossible to receive unmixed pleasures without knowing natural science [*physiologia*]."[26]

Study of nature, Lucretius elaborates, frees the mind from "terror of the mind [...] and gloom" (6.39). We can call this a "negative" reward. Study is needed to free us from false beliefs built up by superstition and religion, by human culture itself (in Greek terms, *nomos* as opposed to *physis*). Fear of death and fear of the gods are the two greatest fears Lucretius wishes to banish, to bring about human happiness. Religion is based on fear of death: a very useful maxim still.

Lucretius teaches about death in order to advise us how to live better. Understanding birth and death are central to philosophy as to religion. But here there is no other world from which birth and death come; no metaphysical causes; no journey of the soul after death to its supposed true home and origin. Instead, know the way things are: be happy knowing we die and do not live forever.

Facts are not "depressing" in themselves; that's the way it is. Our mind can attain truths of eternity (atoms), and be free from fear, from superstition and convention,[27] free of pain. It is better to refer to the Epicurean goal, the untroubled mental state of *ataraxia*, as peacefulness rather than "pleasure".

---

25 Translations by Smith 1992.

26 Epicurus, *Principal Doctrines* 12 (Diog. Laert. 10.143), in *Epicurus Reader*, ed. and trans. Inwood and Gerson, 33. Smith, *Lucretius*, 2001, xxiii; Brague, *The Wisdom*, 38.

27 Lucian's 2nd century AD satirical essay "Alexander or the False Prophet" describes the actual debunking of a fraud by an Epicurean (Lucian himself; his addressee Celsus may, arguably, very well be the same Celsus who wrote the attack on Christianity known from Origen's reply).

Ultimately the Epicurean achieves a calm state of mind, untroubled even by the need to study or investigate or know more. Seen in this way, knowledge sounds like Wittgenstein's concluding image of the ladder.[28] What use will it be when we get to the goal? Epicurus says: if we had no fears, we wouldn't need natural science.[29] The gods serve as a model. The gods' calm peaceful bliss does not seem to involve knowing things like the good scientific truths that people must study. They have static minds, with no desire, not even desire for knowledge, and that state is available to us. We must consider the implications of this.

Some scholars argue that if it were not necessary to remove the errors caused by culture, people would not need knowledge. Perhaps people originally lived in a blissful state of nature, which we aim to recover. In other words, knowledge would not be part of a simple happy life. Nussbaum takes this line. However, she ignores the fact that Lucretius imagines that humans naturally live in a state of fear of the world. She applies Aristotelian terminology to Epicurean ethics, characterizing its goal as a flourishing life, with "unimpeded functioning", "the unimpeded activity of the natural condition".[30] Reason, I think, is a loser here. If "a certain sort of reasoning [...] is included as part of the end", she likewise imagines this to be a practical reason, "closely tied to bodily functions" (*Therapy*, 109).

Is knowledge purely instrumental, a means to something else, such as practical activity? I think not.[31] Practical activity involves things like the manipulation of matter and the struggle to survive, and this is also the realm of political activity, whereas scientific truths lead us to a favorable mental state. It leads to a better *type* of action, such as conversation among friends (a high Epicurean value), as opposed to actions springing from excessive desire (such as

---

28 "He must so to speak throw away the ladder, after he has climbed up on it" (Wittgenstein, *Tractatus*, Proposition 6:54).

29 Epicurus, *Principal Doctrines* 11 (Diog. Laert. 10.142), in *Epicurus Reader*, ed. and trans. Inwood and Gerson, 33.

30 Nussbaum, *Therapy*, 109. The latter phrase is from Aristotle, and "flourishing" is commonly used to explain Aristotle's *eudaimonia* (or "happiness"). Diskin Clay ("Review") justly criticizes Nussbaum for describing Epicurus's happiness as "flourishing", and for ignoring Epicurean science except for medicine (and psychotherapy, her main concern). In general, she wishes to defend emotions and the body ("Epicurus finds truth in the body", 110; this is trite). John Cottingham (*Philosophy and the Good Life*, 59) notes that Nussbaum wishes to argue that Epicureanism makes for healthier emotions, thus downplaying the traditional confrontation of reason and desire. Another limitation appears: she equates "a passion for true philosophy" with "a love of arguments" (*Therapy*, 154). Scholars make their subjects like themselves.

31 See also note 40 below, for the Epicurean criticism of the Stoics' reliance on a political metaphor for the universe.

---

war or avarice). The therapeutic Epicurean ideal of happiness can benefit every human, yet it seems like a rather remote philosophical goal. We must discuss this a little more and take it to a higher level. At issue here is whether human beings are entirely part of the forces of nature, or not.

KNOWLEDGE SAVES (II): GODLIKE CONTEMPLATION

Epicurean scientific knowledge provides a positive reward; it is good in itself and not just as a means to attain better goals in the competitive arena of life. Knowledge provides the only salvation. Contemplation might even (arguably) make us godlike. Lucretius several times describes Epicurus as a god (5.6–8, 19, 51).[32] Metrodorus, one of Epicurus's closest associates, says, "although you are mortal by nature [...], you have ascended, in our discussions of nature, to the infinite and the eternal".[33] How is this possible in a materialist philosophy in which nothing exists but eternal atoms and the void, and even gods consist of atoms?

In philosophical contemplation the mind rises above the realm of matter and becoming. We can see this somewhat mystical notion implicit in Lucretius. We can use this notion to explain how he means Epicurus is like a god and what that teaches all of us.

Lucretius describes Epicurus as a hero who both mastered the laws of nature and went beyond: "his mind's might and vigor prevailed, and on he marched far beyond the blazing battlements of the world, in thought and understanding journeying all through the measureless universe" (1.69–74). With his mind Epicurus travelled beyond our world. That's where the gods dwell (in the spaces between worlds). He was able to achieve a position from which he could look down: "nothing is more blissful than to occupy the heights effectively fortified by the teaching of the wise, tranquil sanctuaries [*templa serena*] from which you can look down" (2.7–9). Religious language is used for new purposes.

This is no mere metaphor. It describes the operation of theoretical mind as opposed to matter. The present world itself will pass away one day—"the walls of the mighty world [...] shall be stormed all around, and shall collapse into crumbling ruin" (2.1144–1145). The sage has already attained a point from

---

32 Plato urged humans to be as godlike as humanly possible, a notion with no small influence on Christian thought (Lenz, "Deification"). In a forthcoming paper with Vishwa Adluri, I argue that the Myth of Er in Plato's *Republic* Book 10 (the story that Socrates claims "will save us too"; see above), exemplifies the mystic knowledge discussed in this section. Konstan (*A Life*, 139) describes Lucretius's transcendental language, also comparing it to the mystery religions, but argues that while it is real for Plato, it is figurative for Lucretius: the curse of being too good a poet?

33 Metrodorus fr. 37 (Koerte), from Clem. Al. *Strom.* 5.138, quoted by Buchheit, "Epicurus' Triumph", 108. See also Clay, "Sources", 33.

which to view that. He sees not only beyond the world but beyond the process of *becoming* itself; "in a certain sense (the sage) stands outside of temporality" (Konstan, *A Life*, xv).[34] The Epicurean may achieve this "sanctuary" (*templa*) as Lucretius has through study of the nature of things (3.15):

> away flee the mind's terrors, the walls of the world open out, I
> see what happens through the whole void: before me appear the
> gods in their majesty, and their peaceful abodes [...] and noth-
> ing at any time impairs their peace of mind. [3.16-18, 23-24]

Several commentators note that the poem uses language evoking the experience of the initiate in a mystery-cult such as the Eleusinian Mysteries, who sees or experiences something and thus (we can say) rises above earthly existence, and receives a reward of a better afterlife. However, many critics find ways to downplay or dismiss this central philosophical theme in Lucretius, partly of course because his system has no place for any afterlife; one common strategy assimilates Lucretius to Roman political culture.[35]

The sage sits in the position of a god, outside our world of becoming, in a blissful state acquired through knowledge of the workings of the world. Through philosophical viewing (*theoria, contemplatio*) he sees the causes of birth and death. That is the essence of the mystical experience, a term deriving from the word for initiates (*mustai*) in the so-called mystery religions who saw a secret religious spectacle. To them, a special afterlife was promised. Lucretius offers this *while alive* to the follower of Epicurus. He presents a highly philosophical ideal of the best human life.

---

34 Courtney, "Epicurus", 257 talks about the dichotomy of Necessity as opposed to freedom of the will.

35 Fowler, *Lucretius*, 50–51, quoted by Konstan, *A Life*, 137. Duncan Kennedy, in Gale, *Lucretius*, 380, notes the "imagery [...] of mystic revelation", but (like most critics) takes this as rhetorical only. The theoretical becomes rhetorical if we only look at language. Equally dismissive of the full philosophical import of this idea, in my opinion, is the trend to read Lucretius in terms of Roman politics or political imagery, *e.g.* to analyze the depiction of the philosopher as a play on praises of a triumphant Greek or Roman general (Buchheit, "Epicurus' Triumph", 121-126, with Gale at Gale, *Lucretius*, 6); see also Buchheit, 109–111 for the "ascent" of Epicurus. Melville notes that "Lucretius reacts like an initiate before the revelation of nature's mysteries" (with reference to 3.28–29), but he then denies the significance of the revelation: "there is a sense in which what he sees is nothing [...] no more than atoms" (Melville, *Lucretius*, 232). More sympathetically, Minadeo properly characterizes Lucretius as possessing "spiritual greatness somehow religious" (Minadeo, *Lyre*, 111). Lucretius's ideals, like those of Socrates and Plato, are higher even than the traditional gods.

John R. Lenz

Lucretius *himself* is not just a poet but a *philosopher*: not only because he presents reasoned arguments, but because he claims that he has reached the insight of a sage. He is not just "learned" in previous Greek lore and poetry, not just a scholarly expounder like his critics.

Hadot explains this insight in another way. We comprehend eternity in an instant.[36] This bears comparison with Spinoza's "intellectual love of God" (where God means the laws of nature), a maxim favored even by the scientifically-minded atheist Bertrand Russell. The co-existence of the material and the quasi-mystical in Lucretius, argued for here, is not as odd as it seems.[37] The physical world obeys natural laws of necessity but our minds, while naturalistic, do not.

This materialistic philosophy does not value the material in the end. Epicureanism is not entirely materialistic when it comes to explaining (or, perhaps, not fully explaining) the mind.[38] The Greek idea of the mind as free from the laws that govern matter gives us the concept of the liberal arts (from Latin "*liber*" "free"). This idea has a long history, traceable from Plato's idea of the soul (the highest part of which is the immortal mind) to the Christian soul. The philosophical ideal holds that the human mind can rise, using reason within rather than revelation from without, to perceive noetically the invisible causes of things. Epicureans call this a godlike state. Epicurus himself promised, "you will live as a god among men" (*Letter to Menoeceus*, 135). Lucretius says, "nothing hinders our living a life worthy of gods" (3.322). Diogenes of Oenoanda spoke this way as well.[39] The gods, even in this system of radical materialism, provide a model of perfection for us. That is one reason Epicurus himself worshipped them.

Science, the rational understanding of "the appearance and law of nature" (*naturae species ratioque*, 6.41), thus promises great rewards for humans, both in practical life in freeing us from fears ("this power wholly belongs to

---

36 Hadot, *Philosophy*, ch. 8, on Goethe and Epicureanism.

37 Stuart Hampshire reckons Lucretius as one of Spinoza's two "intellectual ancestors" (*Spinoza*, 173). Compare Ernst Cassirer on Giordano Bruno: "This doctrine was the first and decisive step towards man's self liberation. […] The infinite universe sets no limits to human reason […]. The human intellect becomes aware of its own infinity" (*An Essay on Man*, as quoted in White, *The Pope*, 71).

38 Long and Sedley (*The Hellenistic Philosophers*, 110) describe it as "an interactionist dualism" (as opposed to a Cartesian dualism). See also Rist, *Epicurus*, 92–94, on the freedom of the mind. The Epicurean "swerve", a difficult concept designed to prevent complete determinism, still does not explain the actions of our minds: if atoms swerve randomly on their own, how do we control this? A different account of non-determinism is presented by Nussbaum (*Therapy*), who argues that Epicureanism develops non-materialistic human values. True, but as noted above, she has a rather practical notion of what these are.

39 Smith, *Lucretius*, 1992, 212 note a; and Smith, *Lucretius*, 2001, xxxi.

reason", 2.53) and more philosophically, in elevating our mind above the vicissitudes of life and the materialistic processes of becoming.

CONCLUSION

Good science makes for better humanities. Lucretius's Epicurean system is very radical, but also timely and timeless. Nature operates impersonally in this extreme materialism. But the philosophy's goals and values are very personal and not materialistic. Paradoxically, what is most personal is timeless: reason, mind.

Science leads to better ethics and fuller humanity based on objective understanding of the workings of the laws of nature throughout the entire universe. The highest development of the human being only comes through awareness of truths of the universe. We are fortified and freed within by this scientific philosophy.

Epicurus counseled avoidance of politics.[40] He was opposed to traditional literary culture (*paideia*) because it kept non-philosophical superstitions alive. This sets him at odds with major trends in the Humanities today, for example in U.S. universities, where many hold that all is politics, meaning especially the identity politics of tribal interest-groups, or that culture trumps biology.

Lucretius is a good humanist because he is a good scientific thinker. Reason is the greatest revelation. All humans share in reason, our best hope. Its goals are high, even transcendent, but this is a democratic elitism. As he writes:

> Piety does not consist in veiling one's head and turning with
> ostentatious frequency to a stone, or in visiting every altar, or
> in prostrating oneself on the ground with outstretched palms
> before the shrines of the gods, or in saturating the sacrificial
> slabs with the blood of four-footed beasts, or in linking vows
> to vows, but rather in possessing the ability to contemplate
> all things with a tranquil mind. [5.1198–1203] [41]

---

40 Interestingly, the Epicurean Diogenes of Oenoanda criticized the Stoic ideal of a
cosmopolis: the Stoics made the world (*cosmos*) a city and thus did not ascend to
blessed tranquility as described above: "what god [...] would have got this idea
that he needed a city and fellow citizens?" (Smith, *Lucretius*, 2001, 141n15). This
reinforces the argument of this paper that the goal is not simply a secular good life.

41 I offer great thanks to Tim Madigan, master humanist, for organizing this event and
inviting me; "of all the things which wisdom provides in order for us to live happily,
there is nothing better, more fruitful, or more pleasant than friendship", Epicurus
wisely said (Cic. *Fin.* 1.20, quoted from Hadot, *Philosophy as a Way of Life*, 125).

SELECT BIBLIOGRAPHY

Asmis, Elizabeth. "Epicurean Poetics". In *Oxford Readings in Ancient Literary Criticism*, edited by A. Laird, 238–266. Oxford: Oxford University Press, 2006.

Aquinas, Thomas. *Summa Theologica*. Vol. 1. Translated by the Fathers of the English Dominican Province. New York: Benzinger Brothers, 1947.

Barash, David P. "C. P. Snow: Bridging the Two-Cultures Divide". *Chronicle of Higher Education* 52, no.14 (November 25, 2005): B10–B11.

Brague, Rémi. *The Wisdom of the World: The Human Experience of the Universe in Western Thought*. Translated by T. L. Fagan. Chicago: University of Chicago Press, 2003.

Buchheit, Vinzenz. "Epicurus' Triumph of the Mind (Lucr. 1.62–79)". In *Lucretius*, Oxford Readings in Classical Studies, edited by Monica Gale, 104–31. Oxford: Oxford University Press, 2007.

Campbell, Gordon. *Lucretius on Creation and Evolution*. Oxford: Oxford University Press, 2003.

Clay, Diskin. "Deep Therapy". Review of *The Therapy of Desire*, by Martha Nussbaum. *Philosophy and Literature* 20, no. 2 (October 1996): 501–505.

——. *Paradosis and Survival: Three Chapters in the History of Epicurean Philosophy*. Ann Arbor: University of Michigan Press, 1998.

——. "The Sources of Lucretius' Inspiration". In *Lucretius*, Oxford Readings in Classical Studies, edited by Monica Gale, 18-47. Oxford: Oxford University Press, 2007.

Cottingham, John. *Philosophy and the Good Life*. Cambridge: Cambridge University Press, 1998.

Courtney, William Leonard. "Epicurus". In *Hellenica*, edited by Evelyn Abbott, 244–265. Port Washington, New York: Kennikat Press, 1971. First published 1880 by Rivingtons, London.

Diogenes Laertius. "Epicurus". In *Lives of Eminent Philosophers*, translated by R. D. Hicks. Vol. 2, rev. ed. London: Heinemann, 1931.

Epicurus. *Letter to Menoeceus*. In *The Epicurus Reader*, edited and translated by Brad Inwood and Lloyd Gerson. Indianapolis: Hackett, 1994.

Fowler, Don P. *Lucretius on Atomic Motion: A Commentary on* De Rerum Natura, *Book Two, Lines 1–332*. Oxford: Oxford University Press, 2002.

Gale, Monica R., ed. *Lucretius*. Oxford Readings in Classical Studies. Oxford: Oxford University Press, 2007.

Hadot, Pierre. *Philosophy as a Way of Life*. Translated by Arnold I. Davidson. Oxford: Blackwell, 2002.

Hampshire, Stuart. *Spinoza and Spinozism*. Oxford: Oxford University Press, 2005.

Harris, Sam. *The End of Faith: Religion, Terror, and the Future of Reason*. New York: Norton, 2004.

Inwood, Brad, and Lloyd Gerson, trans. and ed. *The Epicurus Reader*. Indianapolis: Hackett, 1994.

Johnson, W. R. *Lucretius and the Modern World*. London: Duckworth, 2000.

Johnson, Monte, and Catherine Wilson. "Lucretius and the History of Science". In *The Cambridge Companion to Lucretius*, 131-148, edited by Stuart Gillespie and Philip Hardie. Cambridge: Cambridge University Press, 2007.

Jones, Howard. *The Epicurean Tradition*. London and New York: Routledge, 1989.

Konstan, David. *A Life Worthy of the Gods: The Materialist Psychology of Epicurus*. Las Vegas: Parmenides Publishing, 2008.

Kovacs, Maureen G., trans. *The Epic of Gilgamesh*. Stanford: Stanford University Press, 1989.

Lenz, John R. "Deification of the Philosopher in Classical Greece". In *Partakers of the Divine Nature: The History and Development of Deification in the Christian Traditions*, edited by M. J. Christensen and J. A. Wittung, 47–67. Madison, New Jersey: Fairleigh Dickinson University Press, 2007.

Long, A. A. "Chance and Laws of Nature in Epicureanism". In *From Epicurus to Epictetus*, 157-177. Oxford: Oxford University Press, 2006.

————, and Sedley, D. N. *The Hellenistic Philosophers*. Vol. 1. Cambridge: Cambridge University Press, 1987.

Lucretius. *De Rerum Natura*. Translated by Martin Ferguson Smith. Indianapolis: Hackett, 2001.

————. *De Rerum Natura*. 2nd ed. Edited and translated by Martin Ferguson Smith. Cambridge, Mass: Harvard University Press, Loeb Classical Library, 1992.

————. *On the Nature of the Universe*. Translated by Ronald Melville. Oxford: Oxford University Press, 1997. Reprint 1999.

Martin, Dale B. *Inventing Superstition: From the Hippocratics to the Christians*. Cambridge, Mass.: Harvard University Press, 2004.

Minadeo, Richard. *The Lyre of Science: Form and Meaning in Lucretius'* De Rerum Natura. Detroit: Wayne State University Press, 1969.

Nussbaum, Martha. *The Therapy of Desire: Theory and Practice in Hellenistic Ethics*. Princeton: Princeton University Press, 1994.

Rist, J. M. *Epicurus: An Introduction*. Cambridge: Cambridge University Press, 1972. Reprint 1977.

Sophocles. *Oedipus the King*. In *Sophocles: The Three Theban Plays*, translated by R. Fagles. New York: Viking Penguin, 1982.

Stove, David. "'I only am escaped alone to tell thee': Epistemology and the Ishmael Effect". In *The Plato Cult and Other Philosophical Follies*, 61–82. Oxford: Blackwell, 1991.

Turner, Frank M. "Lucretius among the Victorians". *Victorian Studies* 16 (1973): 329–348.

White, Michael. *The Pope and the Heretic*. New York: William Morrow, 2002.

Wilson, Catherine. *Epicureanism at the Origins of Modernity*. Oxford: Oxford University Press, 2008.

Wittgenstein, Ludwig. *Tractatus Logico-Philosophicus*. New York: Harcourt, Brace & Co., 1922.

Dane R. Gordon

The topic of death is only one of several discussed by Lucretius in his *De Rerum Natura*. The infinity of the universe, the relation between mind and soul, and the development of human society are among them. But death is of central importance to Lucretius and to the teacher he followed, Epicurus.

Their motivation was practical. They cared for people and wanted to help them. They wanted to help them overcome their fear of death and of what might happen after they had died.

To both philosophers religious superstition was needless and self destructive. Lucretius's intention, following Epicurus, was to reveal it for what it was. At the beginning of his *De Rerum* Lucretius applauds Epicurus who, when all could see "that human life lay groveling ignominiously in the dust, crushed beneath the grinding weight of superstition" was "the first who dared to lift mortal eyes to challenge it" (*DRN* 1.62–67).[1] Through him, "superstition is flung down and trampled underfoot" (1.78).

Lucretius was not just against religion; he appeared to have had an intense animosity toward it. His description of Agamemnon's sacrifice of his daughter Iphigenia in order to obtain a favorable wind for the fleet's expedition to Troy is written with controlled rage. Few indictments are as powerful.

This dreadful act was the result of superstition, itself the result of ignorance. The phenomena people did not understand, such as earthquakes and violent storms, they ascribed to the gods. Only as people enlarged their understanding of the natural world could they free themselves from their superstitious fear. Hence the title of his book, *The Nature of Things*. Lucretius would demonstrate that all events have physical causes; divine intervention is not involved.

Yet, even if people accept that, they may still be afraid. Many of their fears will be eliminated, but not all. If the universe is only physical, if there are no gods, what happens when we die? Do we vanish? A fearful thought to many. In a naturalistic world we still may be appalled by the thought of our dissolution.

Lucretius therefore presents two arguments, an extended argument against supernaturalism which is the substance of his book, and a brief argument to deal with the fear of death. In this he follows Epicurus who proposed his own brief argument.

---

1   The M. F. Smith 2001 prose translation of *De Rerum Natura* is used throughout.
    Bibliographic information for all references can be found in the Select
    Bibliography at the end of this essay.

Both arguments are unpersuasive. It is possible that Lucretius may have been aware of the problem that exists within what Epicurus wrote, and endeavored to avoid it.

Here is Epicurus's well-known advice about death as expressed in his *Letter to Menoeceus.* "Accustom thyself to believe that death is nothing to us […], seeing that, when we are, death is not come, and, when death is come we are not." (10.124–126)

Apart from religious beliefs about the afterlife, the second part of the argument is obviously true. When we are dead how can anything mean anything to us? We can't be afraid, we don't exist. But the first part of the argument, that death is nothing to us because when we are, death is not come, is open to question. Simplistically, when we are living we are not dead. It does not follow, however, that while we are living death is nothing to us. Psychologically and emotionally, death is part of life in powerful ways, some as simple a matter as looking out for traffic when we cross the road. If we're careless about it we can be knocked down and killed. We teach our children, "Always look both ways".

Literature is filled with references to death: Virginia Woolf's essay *The Death of a Moth,* in which she compares the struggle of a moth against death with the human struggle; Emily Dickinson's poem "Because I could not stop for death / He kindly stopped for me". We often do live our lives as if death were no part of them. But it is, and it will at some point stop for us. A recent issue of the *New York Times Book Review* included an essay with the title "Death: Bad?" It reviews a new book by Simon Critchley: *Book of Dead Philosophers.* According to Critchley, "What defines bourgeois life in the West today is our pervasive dread of death".[2] After two thousand three hundred years Epicurus's remedy seems not to have worked.

Lucretius avoids Epicurus's problem by not making the claim that when we are death is not. He appeals to reasonableness or common sense. We know nothing about our non-existence before we were born and that does not trouble us. Why should our non-existence after we die be something we're afraid of? He writes:

> Look back now and consider how the bygone ages of eternity
> that elapsed before our birth were nothing to us. Here, then,
> is a mirror in which nature shows us the time to come after
> our death. Do you see anything fearful in it? Do you perceive
> anything grim? Does it not appear more peaceful than
> peaceful sleep? [3.972–977]

(Several passages anticipate this argument in Book 3: 830–840, 868, 910, 928.)

---

2   Jim Holt, review of Simon Critchley.

This has become known as the symmetry argument. The condition of one state is so similar to the condition of the other that if the first is "nothing to us", so should the second. Mikel Burley writes,

> Just as, before we existed we were nothing, so, after we have ceased to exist, will we be nothing again, and since we care nothing (and are *right* to care nothing) about our former non-existence, so should we, on pain of inconsistency, care nothing about our forthcoming non-existence. [Burley, "Lucretius' Symmetry Argument", 329]

One wonders how influential consistency is for a person who is afraid of death. Yet Lucretius is correct, our pre-natal non-existence seldom if ever bothers us. Do we ever even think about it? We do think about our physical death. When we compare that with our present life the contrast is stark, nothingness set against the vitality of being alive, the theme of Woolf's essay and Dickinson's poem.

Regarding death, we cannot avoid it; but unlike pre-natal non-existence, we have some control over when it happens. Apart from the unexpected onset of a disease or an accident, we can increase our life span by taking reasonable precautions, exercising the body, keeping the mind agile and refraining from potentially harmful habits. According to Seneca, life is long if you know how to use it (*On the Shortness of Life*, 3). These practices may not banish the fear, but they may alleviate it so that it is not as painful and destructive of our present life.

Most persons would agree, we can alleviate our fear. That, in fact, is the offer of religion. However, a person's fear of death will not always be the same, and the fear of death felt by one person may be different from the fear of death felt by another. This follows from the intensely personal nature of each person's fear, which both Epicurus and Lucretius overlook except for the descriptions in *De Rerum* of individuals whom Lucretius may have known who were afraid of death. Even there he writes generally of such fear as if it were of one kind for all people, but that is a lacuna in his discussion of this topic. Death is treated impersonally in medical literature and often by philosophers, but it is not impersonal.

At one extreme of the spectrum of fear is what one might describe as the horror of death. George Cruikshank's illustration of Fagin in the condemned cell (Dickens, *Oliver Twist*, facing page 329) is as dramatic a representation of such a horror as I know. Given the character of his life as created by Charles Dickens, Fagin's horror would have persisted until he was strangled by the hangman's rope. Dietrich Bonhoeffer, condemned by the Nazis to be hanged for his complicity in a plot to assassinate Hitler, feared death, but being ordered to the scaffold, he composed himself with prayer and, according to an eye witness, went to his death bravely and calmly. At the other extreme from horror is the mother of a woman whom I know. She is over a hundred, in moderate health, and told her daughter recently that she is ready to die. She has lived a long life and, others say, a good life. She is not afraid of death. At this point she waits for it, even will welcome it.

As in the case of Bonhoeffer, it is not only that there are different degrees of fear, but that a person can move from one to the other. We assume it to be from greater fear to lesser fear, but not always. A woman who did not fear death may come to fear it greatly when it approaches because of the young children whom she will leave without their mother.

I have noticed in Lucretius works that those who fear death are represented as passive before it, death confronts them and they die. Does that have to be? We might think of Norman Cousins's heroic refusal to give in to death.[3] He extended his life for several years by the "medicine", as he described it, of laughter!

Our pre-natal non-existence cannot be changed. It has happened, we cannot alter when it was as we didn't exist. Yet we could argue that there are ways that prenatal non-existence, although it cannot be changed, may nevertheless be influential in our lives. The influence however is not in the state of non-existence but when it ended, that is, when we were born. A man born in the UK in 1920 would be among the first to be drafted when Britain declared war on Germany in 1939. He might reflect, as he waits to be evacuated from the beaches at Dunkirk, that had he been born even five years later he would not be in the army at that time in imminent danger of violent death. Had he been born in 1930 he would have escaped the war altogether.

Such reasoning is criticized by Thomas Nagel. He writes, "We cannot say that the time prior to a man's birth is a time in which he would have lived had he been born not then but earlier. For aside from the brief margin permitted by premature labor, he could not have been born earlier; anyone born substantially earlier than he was would have been someone else" (Nagel, "Death", 8). Symmetry between pre-natal and posthumous non-existence cannot be in that instance because the two experiences involve different persons.

Lucretius states as much in his *De Rerum*. Discussing the materiality of the soul which is destroyed with the destruction of the body he writes:

> If in the course of time all our component atoms should be reassembled after our death and restored again to their present positions, so that the light of life was given to us a second time, even that eventuality would not affect us in the least, once there had been a break in the chain of consciousness. [3.845]

---

3   Norman Cousins was editor of *The Saturday Review*.

When once the physical continuity of a person is interrupted, that person is gone; any reconstitution of the parts results in a different person.

Yet it is possible to reflect upon the date of our birth, rehearsing the consequences to ourselves of an earlier or later birth without needing to consider whether we would be different people. What is important is that such reflections might influence our life. Having been spared the war, a person born in 1930 might decide to take life more seriously, knowing that several of his slightly older friends were killed. He might decide to go into politics to help prevent another war, or become a physician to help those who were wounded in the war. He would, of course, not be concerned with his non-existence before he was born, but he would be concerned with when he was born. To that extent there is perhaps an equivalence between such considerations toward the time of our birth and considerations of when we die. The thought of our death may spur us on to accomplish as much as we can while we are alive, as the time of our birth may spur us on to accomplish all we can in the circumstances of life in which the date of our birth has placed us.

Being aware of when we were born may not change this, yet it may change our attitude toward life, from regarding it as a given to appreciating it as a gift. We do not have to be religious to do this, but to regard our life as something unique to us and precious can transform it from a sometimes burdensome continuum to a meaningful responsibility to ourselves and others.

A special case in the context of this discussion is the Hindu doctrine of reincarnation, which one writer on the topic has described as "not so much a revealed doctrine as a self evident fact of existence" (Zaehner, *Hinduism*, 4).

A Hindu may not know the details of the life he lived before his present life, but he knows that there was a life. He knows that the cycle of birth and re-birth goes back to the beginning of existence, and will continue unless the individual finds escape or *moksha*. Hence there was a previous life, and he can surmise from his present condition what kind of life it may have been. Were he to conclude that his present unhappiness is the result of how he lived previously, that is likely to affect how he lives now in anticipation of the kind of life allotted to him in the future. Here is an equivalency of a different kind, not equivalent oblivion but equivalent concern with the conduct of life.

Lucretius makes a brief reference to India in his *De Rerum* (2.534) but indicates no familiarity with Indian religion and philosophy. The teaching of Cārvāka, a school of philosophy which began during the period of the Vedas (ca. 1500 BC), long before Epicurus and Lucretius, could have been of interest to Lucretius. It is a materialistic philosophy that rejects all forms of religion, and regards pleasure and pain as the central facts of life. After death is nothing. Reading from the *Sarva-Darśana-Saṁgraha*, a Cārvāka text: "The only end of man is enjoyment produced by sensual pleasures." These pleasures, however, are modest. "The wise should enjoy the pleasures of this world through the proper visible means of agriculture, keeping cattle, trade, political administration […]"

(Radhakrishnan, *Soucebook*, 228–230), not unlike the character of Epicurean life as described by Diogenes Laertius.

Perhaps we have strayed too far from Lucretius, but I think that given the interconnectedness of the world of thought, still to be more fully appreciated, an awareness of parallel philosophical ideas from different times and places can sharpen our understanding of them all.

The symmetry passage in *De Rerum* receives a great deal of attention, but it is only a small part of a long disquisition at the end of Book 3, in which Lucretius presents a passionate and cumulatively powerful argument against the two fears, death and the gods.

> But what of Cerberus and the Furies and the realm destitute of light? What of Tartarus vomiting waves of fearful fumes from its jaws? These terrors do not exist and cannot exist anywhere at all. But in life people are tortured by a fear of punishment as cruel as their crimes, and by the atonement for their offenses—the dungeon, the terrible precipitation from the Rock, stripes, executioners, the execution cell, pitch, red-hot plates, torches. Even though these horrors are absent, the mind, conscious of its guilt and fearfully anticipating the consequences, pricks itself with goads and sears itself with scourges. It fails to see how there can be an end to its afflictions, or a limit to its punishment; indeed it is afraid that its sufferings may increase in death. In short, fools make a veritable hell of their lives on earth. [3.1010–1025]

I quote this long passage for two reasons. It illustrates the compliment given to Lucretius by J. D. Duff, a 19th century Cambridge classicist. He writes, "It has often struck me that his genius is akin to Milton" ("Introduction", xx). In this passage and others, such as his description of the woolly flocks of sheep cropping the glad pastures on a hill, the poet seems to dominate the philosopher (*DRN* 2.320). Yet the passage is part of the claim Lucretius makes that as we acquaint ourselves with the physical world we will banish our superstitions about the supernatural and, as a consequence, our fear of death, a leading motivation for Epicurus's physical theories and, hence, Lucretius's great poem. The argument is unconvincing. *The Center for Theology and Natural Sciences*, an international organization whose members are mostly scientists, demonstrates that knowledge of science does not drive out religious belief. But Lucretius makes the point, denied by the Roman Catholic Church up to the time of Galileo, that we must study the physical universe in order to understand it.

In fairness, however, to both Epicurus and Lucretius, they lived in a pre-scientific world that was deeply superstitious. Our Western society probably cannot understand the extent to which this affected the thought of the average person then, who would have found atheism incomprehensible. Epicurus's and Lucretius's remedies for the fear of death would become effective only very slowly in that environment, even though Epicureanism had many followers.

Yet, before we congratulate ourselves on having gone beyond that, consider the strong negative reaction to the publication of Charles Darwin's *Origin of Species* in 1859, one hundred and fifty years ago. Consider the continuing strong and influential objections expressed now, and the influence of these on the teaching of science in schools.

The work of Epicurus and Lucretius is relevant in this respect; it is not only a scientific and philosophical curiosity of the past, but an issue of current debate.

I have a few additional observations, direct and indirect, about Lucretius's discussion of the topic of death. For instance, the examples he uses in the last third or so of Book 3 to illustrate the irrationality and foolishness of the fear of death, in my opinion are overdone and out of touch with how most people behave. He presents a person who bemoans and beweeps the prospect of death (3.935), and then an older person, more advanced in years, also bewailing and bemoaning the approach of death. "Stop sniveling, you dolt!" writes Lucretius (3.954). He writes disparagingly about those who are angry because after death they "will either rot in the grave or be devoured in flames or the jaws of wild beasts" (3.871).

These really are caricatures, even though based probably on people whom Lucretius had met. One might suppose that all Roman society was terrified by the fear of death. Hardly. What would Roman soldiers at that time have thought if they'd read it? Menander's plays were written in the third century BC, when just those fears were rampant, but they do not show up in his plays, which are about ordinary families with ordinary domestic problems, often ridiculous, generally funny. A photograph from the Second World War shows General Eisenhower with his troops shortly before they invaded France. The men were animated and smiling, though many would be dead a few hours later, and they knew it. Lucretius's method here is to draw general conclusions from specific instances. It's often done, and is often effective, but it's a vulnerable kind of argument.

Another observation is that while Lucretius's work provides prescient hypotheses of the nature and operation of the physical universe, and while his materialistic ethic and his emphasis upon the value of this life now is courageous, his sensitivity to the larger metaphysical and personal implications of his teaching is disappointing. Mentioned earlier, it is not the case that when we are alive death is of no concern, as Epicurus wrote. We are concerned, often philosophically, asking questions that are not solved as readily as Lucretius, following Epicurus, claims. Our fear of death waxes and wanes through different experiences and different stages of life. Lucretius gives little attention to the depths and complexity of such fears and the active role they play, not always negative, in people's lives.

Have I missed the point? Lucretius set out to describe a physical universe. That explanation itself would, he believed, relieve people of their igno-

---

rance, the source of their fear, and provide them with peace of mind. Yet the nature of things includes the nature of human inquisitiveness, which invites questions about what he has written.

Lucretius writes, "nothing ever springs miraculously out of nothing" (1.150). Later he writes, "particles of matter are supplied from below, darting out of infinite space" (1.995). Is that a contradiction?

According to him, the source of the particles is infinite space, but what is that? Certainly it is a useful postulate; science does not explain itself, but do we stop there? If Lucretius uses "infinite space" as a *terminus a quo* without further explanation, does that affect his dismissal of religious belief as superstition?

A contemporary scientist has written, "The rich complexity of creation demands an account of the world which [...] must accommodate within its metaphysical embrace both the constituent insights of elementary particle physics and also the integrating insights of aesthetic and religious experience" (Polkinghorne, *Science and Creation*, 69). Given his premises, Lucretius could not do that.

Throughout his work he is critical of religion. His description of the sacrifice of Iphigenia is as damning an indictment as can be found. Religion is responsible for many dreadful things. Why do people believe?

His claim that that is easy to explain is questionable (5.1109). Although in some respects, he is correct. Humans look for a power beyond themselves, often for selfish reasons, and thereby become prey to religious delusions.

What is not easy to explain is the universal impetus towards religious belief, even when fear is not an issue, even if the nature of natural phenomena is understood. I have come to feel that *De Rerum Natura*, great as it is, stops short. It does not probe beyond the physical. If that is all Lucretius intended, however, the objection is unreasonable. Lucretius's commitment to materialistic explanations is an ontological decision which, if it is to be philosophical and not theological (a charge made against Epicurus), should be open to debate.

If the problem of evil is that the gods whom people trust fail them, the problem with the problem of evil is that even then they still turn to the gods (Gordon, *Feeling*, 65). Either this is an example of human foolishness, or of depths to be found in men and women despite themselves. But these may be unreasonable objections. Lucretius was a poet. We don't fault Tennyson because, in his poem "Lucretius", he did not question St. Jerome.

At the beginning of *De Rerum* Lucretius pays a noble tribute to his mentor, Epicurus, for how he challenged the gods, faced them down and lived life independently of religious superstition. It takes a certain type of courage to live in a world that one regards as impersonal, nothing other than the physical. Lucretius based his life on that. He died young, at age 44. According to some his poem was unfinished, although not all agree with that.[4] An ancient tradition, preserved by St. Jerome, probably not true, is that Lucretius was subject to fits of

---

4   Gillespie and Mackenzie, "Lucretius", 309. See also Smith, "Introduction", xi–xiii.

---

insanity and died by his own hand. If true, did he lose faith in his own teaching? We don't know at all. We know only what he wrote, which he may never have repudiated. "If human beings would guide their lives by true principles, great wealth consists in living on little with a contented mind" (5.1118). Surely, a contended mind is one that has come to grips with and overcome the fear of death.

SELECT BIBLIOGRAPHY

Burley, Mikel. "Lucretius' Symmetry Argument and the Determinacy of Death". *The Philosophical Forum* 38 (2007): 327–341.

Dickens, Charles. *The Adventures of Oliver Twist*. London: Chapman and Hall, Crown Edition, 1895.

Duff, J. D. "Introduction". In *On the Nature of Things*, by Lucretius. Edited by Duff. Translated by H. A. J. Munro. London: G. Bell and Sons, 1914.

Epicurus. *Letter to Menoeceus*. In *Lives of the Eminent Philosophers*, by Diogenes Laertius, vol. 2, bk. 10. Translated by R. D. Hicks. Cambridge, Mass.: Harvard University Press, Loeb Classical Library, 1931.

Gillespie, Stuart and Donald Mackenzie. "Lucretius and the Moderns" In *The Cambridge Companion to Lucretius*, edited by Gillespie and Philip Hardie. Cambridge: Cambridge University Press, 2007.

Gordon, Dane R. *A Feeling Intellect and a Thinking Heart*. Lanham, Maryland: The University Press of America, 2002.

Holt, Jim. "Death: Bad?" Review of *Book of Dead Philosophers*, by Simon Critchley. *New York Times Book Review*, February 15, 2009.

Lucretius. *On the Nature of Things*. Translated by Martin Ferguson Smith. Indianapolis: Hackett, 2001.

Nagel, Thomas. "Death". In *Mortal Questions*, 1–10. Cambridge: Cambridge University Press, 1979.

Polkinghorne, John, FRS. *Science and Creation: The Search for Understanding*. London: SPCK Publishing, 1988.

Radhakrishnan, Sarvepalli, and Charles A. Moore. *A Sourcebook in Indian Philosophy*. Princeton: Princeton University Press, 1967.

Seneca. *On the Shortness of Life*. In *Moral Essays*, vol. 2, bk. 10.3. Translated by John W. Basore. Cambridge, Mass.: Harvard University Press, Loeb Classical Library, 1932.

Smith, Martin Ferguson. Introduction to *On the Nature of Things*, by Lucretius. Indianapolis: Hackett, 2001.

Zaehner, R. C. *Hinduism*. New York: Oxford University Press, 1966.

David B. Suits

Lucretius, like his master Epicurus, was an atomist. The entire universe was thought to be an infinity of atoms moving in an infinity of space in an infinity of time. Humans too—bodies and souls—are nothing but elaborate and peculiar collections of atoms. Death is the dispersal of these atoms.

Although most people fear death and wish to avoid death, in Book 3 of *De Rerum Natura*, Lucretius makes the Epicurean pronouncement that such a fear is ultimately unfounded—that if we understand death correctly, we will discover that it is "nothing to us"[1] (*DRN* 3.830).[2] Shortly thereafter (and parenthetically to his main argument), Lucretius entertains the thought that it is possible that we will have a postmortem re-existence. (An unstated implication is that perhaps we have had prior lives.) The issue is important, because if re-existence is possible, then our souls (spirits, minds) might not be mortal after all, and people who fear annihilation might have some measure of hope. But Lucretius can reject the idea of past or future lives for three kinds of reasons. (1) He has already (3.425–829) presented many arguments in favor of the materiality and the mortality of the soul (or against the immortality of the soul); and if death is the dissolution of both the body and the soul, then there is no longer a body or a soul that can have a next life. (2) The internal evidence—our lack of memories of any prior life—is against the possibility of past lives (see especially 3.670–697 and 3.741–753). (3) But it is a third argument which I want to consider at length. As we will see, it relies in part on internal evidence (that we cannot remember past lives), but it adds a new consideration. At 3.847–861

---

1 The *De Rerum Natura*'s 1992 prose translation by Rouse and Smith is used throughout. Bibliographic information for all references can be found in the Select Bibliography at the end of this essay.

2 That is, the prospect of your own annihilation ought to be of no concern to you. (Of course, your death might be important to others.) Epicurus's original argument, in his *Letter to Menoeceus*, can be represented in this way: (1) All good and bad consist in sense experience. (2) Death is the destruction of the person; i.e., after death we do not exist. (3) Therefore, there can be no sense experience for dead people. (4) Therefore, death cannot be of any concern to dead people. (5) So long as we are living, we are not dead. (6) So our own death cannot be affecting us now. (7) As for the prospect of our future death, it is silly to worry or be concerned about something that we know will give us no pain when it occurs. (8) Therefore, death does not concern the living. (9) Therefore, death is nothing to us.

Lucretius takes a kind of pragmatic approach, concluding that any hypothesis of multiple existences ought to be, like death itself, nothing to us.

RECOMBINATION

Although we usually think of death as permanent, Lucretius wondered about the possibility that all of a person's atoms which were dispersed at death might later on accidentally recombine in precisely the way they had been just prior to death. Here is the relevant passage:

> Even if time should gather together our matter after death and bring it back again as it is now placed, and if once more the light of life should be given to us, yet it would not matter one bit to us that even this had been done, when the recollection of ourselves has once been broken asunder. And even now we are not concerned at all about any self which we have been before, nor does any anguish about it now touch us. For when you look back upon all the past expanse of measureless time, and think how various are the motions of matter, you may easily come to believe [*facile hoc accredere possis*] that these same seeds of which now we consist have been often before placed in the same arrangement they now are in. And yet we cannot call that back by memory; for in between has been cast a stoppage of life, and all the motions have wandered and scattered afar from those sensations. [3.847–861][3]

---

3 The Rouse/Smith translation renders *facile hoc accredere possis* (3.856) as "you may easily come to believe [that recombinations have occurred before]", while Warren ("Lucretian *Palingenesis*", 499) offers "you may easily understand [that recombinations have occurred before]", and he says that Epicurean cosmology—unlimited atoms moving in unlimited space in unlimited time—requires that atoms will recombine in the same ways over and over again. But Warren is not correct. Lucretius ought to be read as claiming that a perfect recombination of the atoms of a person (or of anything at all) is only a possibility, not a necessity. This reading is justified on four grounds: (1) Lucretius introduces the passage with a compound conditional: "even if […] and if […]", so that the whole discussion of recombination is mere hypothesis. (2) Lucretius's *accredere* should be read not as "understand" but as "believe". The difference can be significant. "Understand" is a success word: you cannot understand that X is true if X really is false; but you can believe that X is true in any case. In the case before us, X happens to be false, because (3) Epicurus himself nowhere claimed that all combinations of atoms must recur, which is just as well, because (4) the logic of endlessness, or the Epicurean cosmology of infinite atoms in infinite space through infinite time,

What are we to make of the possibility that a person's dispersed atoms could recombine as they had been before death? There are two important kinds of issues that can be raised here: ontological issues about whether an apparently recreated person is really the same as the earlier version, and practical issues—that is, prudential issues—of whether the ontological issues should matter. The ontological issues divide into three. (1) We can imagine the very same atoms being put back together in the same arrangement as before. That is what Lucretius was talking about; let us call it "recurrence". Or (2) we can add to Lucretius's speculations by imagining different atoms being put into the same arrangement as the original atoms had been in; let us call this "cloning". Finally, (3) we could imagine that there is something essential or central to a person that somehow manages to live multiple lives or lifetimes (although it is not clear what such a something could be, at least in Lucretius's materialist view; it could not be the soul atoms, because they are dispersed at death along with the rest of the person's atoms). Let us call this "rebirth".[4]

When modern philosophers talk about issues such as recurrence or cloning or rebirth, they are most likely interested in questions about personal identity—whether certain kinds of changes do or do not give rise to a different person. We will touch on such issues below. But notice that in the quote above, Lucretius does not make a claim that personal identity would be either lost or preserved on account of the dispersal and reconnection of atoms. He approaches the issue with a different motive, which appears in his comment in the first sentence: "it would not matter to us one bit". He does not say "it would not be us", nor "recombination would not preserve identity". Beyond an earlier protracted argument that the soul, like all other collections of atoms,

does not guarantee that every possible combination will occur even once, let alone that every actual combination will recur again and again. Numbers provide a convenient analog: a sequence of numbers can be infinite even though not all digits show up (e.g., the decimal expansion of 1/3); and there is no guarantee that an arbitrary sequence of digits that occurs in, say, the endless expansion of π will be repeated even once, let alone an unlimited number of times.

4   Consider another possibility: the vital processes of the person are suspended (or at least slowed to a virtual stop), so that we could say that the person is dead; at some later time the vital processes are restarted. Would this be a case of death and re-existence that makes use of the person's own atoms? Lucretius might say that the question of re-existence should not arise in such a case, because the claim of death would be incorrect. While individual atoms are always, of necessity, in rapid motion, it might be possible to slow down organic processes by slowing down the relative motions of collections of atoms. But as long as the collections of body atoms continue to contain the soul atoms, then the person continues to exist, and the state of suspension should be called just that (or perhaps some kind of coma), but not death.

is destroyed at death, Lucretius does not explicitly deal with the ontological issues of personal identity.[5] That is to say, he does not explicitly argue that an atomically reconstituted person cannot be the original person, or that a reconstituted mind or soul cannot be identical to the original. Rather, Lucretius says "it would not matter". He reminds us that we have no recollection of any earlier life, and he uses that fact to make a very practical point (typical of Epicureans)—not about what is or is not a metaphysical truth, but rather about what should or should not be of any concern to us. I will call this *Lucretius's Key*. It is a version of Epicurus's advice (*Letter to Pythocles*, in Diog. Laert., 10.85) that the practical purpose for investigation and explanation is satisfaction (peace of mind, or serenity).

So let us see how this practical stance—Lucretius's Key—allows us to deal with the three ontological issues of recurrence, cloning, and rebirth. Let us first deal with the ontological version that Lucretius would have little sympathy with, namely, rebirth—the re-existence of a self of some sort (we will have to interpret that notion very broadly) from one life to another. The reason to consider the case of rebirth first is because it will illustrate Lucretius's insight at work on an old idea that is familiar to us all.

REBIRTH

According to much popular Indian thought, at death an individual soul is transferred from one life form to another.[6] But even doctrines (such as Buddhism) that say that there are no permanent souls—no substantial essences—can nevertheless claim that there is *samsāra*, which is a "wandering" (transmigration, or death and rebirth, or continuation somehow) of personality or character. According to Buddhism, one is caught in a cycle of birth and rebirth into lives in which one's desires and ignorance produce suffering. Of moral importance is *karma*, an application of the law of cause and effect in the moral realm, whereby one is what one has made oneself, and one will be what one will have made oneself.[7] Your character follows your actions (and/or intentions); you bring on your own unhappiness or your own salvation. That is, moral consequences can be traced back to your prior actions in this or a previous life or lives, and your present actions will have moral consequences for you in this life or a future life or lives.

---

5   That earlier argument includes a very brief denial that identity could be preserved across lives (3.677–678).

6   But not just Indian thought. Doctrines of metempsychosis can be found virtually everywhere. In the early philosophical West there were Pythagoras, Empedocles and Plato. And Stoicism, which developed at about the same time as Epicureanism, espoused a version of transmigration.

7   In Jainism, karma is thought to be a subtle form of matter that can contaminate the nonmaterial soul.

But here is a question that I take to be in the spirit of Lucretius's Key: I can easily understand how various desires can bring about suffering, and how restructuring these desires and my attitudes about myself and the world can eliminate the suffering. (The Epicureans—and the Stoics too—had such a view.) But that is to speak of what I know to be my desires and my experiences. What I do not understand is how the hypothesis of the cycle of birth and rebirth could make any difference to me. What is any past version of me to myself now? Suppose there were many previous versions of me; or else suppose that this present version is unique. What difference could that make to me now, if I have no knowledge or memories of any previous life? If there *were* such memories, they might make a difference because I might learn from them; I could relate some present suffering or present pleasure to past actions, decisions, desires, or habits. In my life I see all sorts of connections between what I do and the pleasure or pain I experience, and so I can learn to restructure my desires and actions. But I do not see what good a transmigrational or rebirth hypothesis does, if my present situation is supposed to be, but is never experienced as, the results of unidentified desires and actions of an alleged past version of me. For all I can know, it was someone or something else, and not a previous version of me, that has brought about my present circumstances.

Even if there were previous versions of me or my character, anything at all that such a previous "self" did or said or desired might, for all I can know, have resulted in the way I am now. If I am suffering, is it because in a previous life I enjoyed chocolate? Or is it because I did not enjoy chocolate? Or is chocolate irrelevant to the explanation? How can I know? Such questions can be raised with regard to my present suffering, in case I am suffering, or my present pleasure, in case I am enjoying something, or my present occupation, life-style, eye color, how much interest I pay for a home mortgage, or whether I am indifferent to basketball. Yet there is no connection that I am aware of between any putative previous lives and my present life. Lucretius's Key therefore recommends that we abandon the rebirth hypothesis—not because it is false, but because it is of no use.[8]

---

8   A. R. Wadia briefly entertains a complaint against a doctrine of reincarnation: if a
     person cannot recall the misdeeds of a past life, then punishment for past misdeeds
     would seem to be ineffective. Wadia dismisses the complaint as "not very convincing":
          Even in our normal life we do not remember everything we experience. It
          would be a calamity if our memory were to be burdened with the recol-
          lection of every little occurrence in our life. It has been wisely said that the
          art of remembering is the art of forgetting. If in one single life the load of
          memory is so unbearable, how much worse would it be if we had to bear
          the burden of remembering the events, however important they might
          have been, in our past life or lives. ["Philosophical Implications", 148]
     It is difficult to assess Wadia's response. He seems to be saying that if in this life we
     do not remember everything, including all our misdeeds, and if we are nevertheless

---

As we saw earlier, Lucretius mentions the possibility of the perfect recombination of all of a person's atoms after having been dispersed at death. If we are concerned about issues of personal identity, then it is not clear how to understand the implications of such an hypothesis. There seems to be no good evidence of our or anyone else's recurrence, so if we want to try to understand how a reconstituted person might be (or not be) the same person as the ante-dispersal person, then we will have to find clues in our appreciation of familiar things that appear to become dispersed and later reconstituted. For example, a jigsaw puzzle, solved once, taken apart, and solved a second time, remains the same puzzle. The internal combustion engine of my automobile, taken apart and put back together again (perhaps with a few replacement parts) is still my engine. But suppose a storm breeds a tornado which soon wanes and seems to disappear. Along the track of the storm a tornado appears again. Is it the first tornado, reconstituted? Or a different one? We do not know exactly how a tornado is formed; we cannot follow the constituent parts and forces with certainty, and so we cannot predict with certainty the appearance of a tornado, and consequently our tendency is to claim that the one is not identical to the other.

Far more difficult, then, would it be to track the dispersal of sub-visible person-parts and put them back together again. We simply have no experiences of this sort.[9] Perhaps we could get some ideas from fiction. *Star Trek* and other science-fiction stories make use of transporter devices that decompose persons (and many other things) and recombine them elsewhere. We are given no good grounds for distinguishing (or having a motive to distinguish) pre-transported persons from post-transported persons, except in a few unusual stories in which a transporter malfunctions,[10] but those exceptions actually serve to

---

held responsible for all that we do, then there is no principled reason not to extend that responsibility to other lifetimes as well. But his response is unconvincing. A more plausible claim would be that a person should not be held morally responsible for actions he cannot remember (even in this life).

Moreover, the doctrine of karma need not be a parallel to juridical ideas of responsibility and punishment. One could say, rather, that karma simply is cause and effect in the moral realm, whereas the use of punishment is a question for social institutions (which may or may not overlap with morality).

In any case, the complaint to which Wadia responds ought not to be confused with the issue I am raising, which is much broader than issues of punishment.

9   An important difference between, on the one hand, puzzles and automobiles, and, on the other hand, tornadoes and persons, is that the former are thought to be static, whereas the latter are said to be dynamic—they are *processes*, and the identity conditions for processes can be very problematic.

10   For examples, "The Enemy Within" from the first season of *Star Trek*, and "Mirror, Mirror" from the second season.

---

reinforce our feelings that a properly functioning transporter does indeed preserve personal identity.

So let us simply stipulate that personal identity is somehow preserved when the very same atoms that were scattered abroad at death are now recombined in exactly the same arrangement that they had prior to death. This is Lucretius's speculation; I have called it "recurrence". But instead of resorting to science fiction, let us resort to one particularly dramatic and well-known way that a person could recur, namely, in the case that everything recurs. As the exemplar of this hypothesis, we will use Nietzsche.

> [Suppose] some day or night a demon were to sneak after you into your loneliest loneliness and say to you, "This life as you now live it and have lived it, you will have to live once more and innumerable times more; and there will be nothing new in it, but every pain and every joy and every thought and sigh and everything immeasurably small or great in your life must return to you—all in the same succession and sequence—even this spider and this moonlight between the trees, and even this moment and I myself. The eternal hourglass of existence is turned over and over, and you with it […]." Would you not throw yourself down and gnash your teeth and curse the demon who spoke thus? Or did you once experience a tremendous moment when you would have answered him, "You are a god, and never have I heard anything more godly." If this thought were to gain possession of you, it would change you, as you are, or perhaps crush you. The question in each and every thing, "Do you want this once more and innumerable times more?" would weigh upon your actions as the greatest stress. Or how well disposed would you have to become to yourself and to life to *crave nothing more fervently* than this ultimate eternal confirmation and seal? [*The Gay Science*, §341]

Nietzsche praises

> the ideal of the most high-spirited, alive, and world-affirming human being who has not only come to terms and learned to get along with whatever was and is, but who wants to have *what was and is* repeated into all eternity, shouting insatiably *da capo*. [*Beyond Good and Evil*, §56]

Elsewhere he says:

> My formula for greatness for a human being is *amor fati*: that
> one wants nothing to be different, not forward, not backward,
> not in all eternity. ["Why I am So Clever", in *Ecce Homo*, §10]

But there are problems with such a view. The first problem is that no
sensible person would actually take the alleged demon at his word. (Is it really a
demon? Most people would suspect that a bad practical joke was afoot. Even if it
is a real demon, you need to know what demons are capable of. And are they to
be trusted? Is this demon telling the truth? How could you possibly know?)

Second, eternal recurrence as a scientific hypothesis seems to have
little to support it. Walter Kaufmann suggests that Nietzsche may have been
influenced by this passage in a book by Heinrich Heine:

> Time is infinite, but the things in time, the concrete bodies, are
> finite. They may indeed disperse into the smallest particles;
> but these particles, the atoms, have their determinate number,
> and the number of the configurations that, all of themselves,
> are formed out of them is also determinate. Now, however
> long a time may pass, according to the eternal laws governing
> the combinations of this eternal play of repetition, all
> configurations that have previously existed on this earth must
> yet meet, attract, repulse, kiss, and corrupt each other again.[11]

The idea embraced by Heine is not unlike the idea dismissed by
Lucretius, and my comments in note 3 above against the necessity of recurrence
apply here as well (even though Heine is supposing that space is finite and that
there is a finite number of particles).

A third problem is that the idea of "eternal recurrence" probably brings
to mind some of our own experiences of events and our own experiences of
their recurrences. Take an unwelcome event: I am waiting in line at some government bureaucracy. Eventually I reach the front, but I am told that I must go
through another line first—and then come back and wait again in this one. It
seems that eternal recurrence would be like having to go from one line to another, waiting for the opportunity to wait—having to do things yet again and
again. Oppressive tedium.

But that is only an initial image drawn from some repetitive experiences,
such that if I thought that they would continue in that way, I would think "O! the
horror!" One can also imagine a repetition of kinds of events one has loved, in

---

11 Kaufmann, *Nietzsche*, 318. The original source is not clear. See Kaufmann's
comments, 318n9.

which case the prospect of recurrence might be greeted with joy.

Yet upon examination, eternal recurrence cannot be like that. In fact, it must necessarily be like nothing at all. Instead of saying that there are events in your life that you might or might not want to repeat, you should say that there are *kinds* of events that would be good (or bad) to repeat. You should not be concerned about a repetition of a particular event in *all its details*, because one of the details was your unawareness of its being a repetition. Waiting in the *next* line is oppressive, not only because waiting in any line can be oppressive, but also because it is added to waiting in the previous line. But if there is an "eternal recurrence of the same", then the recurrence cannot be in my experience. To experience recurrence is to experience the *again*, and that is precisely what I cannot experience if everything occurs exactly as before.

So there is a problem with eternal recurrence; it is a sibling of the problem with rebirth, and it is identified by Lucretius's Key: what difference could it make for me? If everything repeated exactly as before, then there would be no way of knowing it, of taking it into account, of its having any effects whatsoever. A perfectly repeated past must be precisely like a non-repeated past.[12]

Harold Alderman says that we are not to take eternal recurrence as a cosmological truth—a fact to be argued for, and for which evidence can be given. It is, rather a belief, a perspective, a

> joyous celebration of a condition which, even if it were not the case, we would have to invent, in order to test the degree of our self-acceptance. Though in a single lifetime one might be said to live many lives, who of us is strong enough to say, "I accept myself even through an eternity of lives"? [...]

> One then gains final admission to Nietzsche's perspective by enacting the difficult soliloquy in which one can freely exult, "Was *that* life? Well then! Once more!" [*Nietzsche's Gift*, 110]

On such a view, eternal recurrence is not to be taken as having a truth value; it has rather a psychological point, namely, to enhance our lives. We will, it is said, be able to take a different view of ourselves if we take Nietzsche's myth in the subjunctive mood: act *as if* eternal recurrence were true.

But it is not clear to me what good that does. Eternal recurrence is an idea which, upon examination, expresses something that cannot possibly matter to us. What, after all, are we supposed to accept, even if only subjunctively?

---

12 Suppose a demon comes to you and asks if you wish a particularly pleasant event repeated. "Yes!" you say, full of the joyousness of your own life. "Very well", says the demon. "How was that? Would you like to repeat it still again?" You will protest that you are still waiting for the first repetition.

Evidently, that things will recur exactly as before. But to be able to say "Was *that* life?", or to love one's fate and be a "world affirming human being [...] shouting insatiably *da capo*", is to be on the outside of one's life, looking back, and this is necessarily impossible to do when it comes to one's whole life. (The best that one can do is to say "Is *this* life? Well then! Continue!")

Alexander Nehamas admits that there could be attitudes to the idea of eternal recurrence other than despair or exhilaration: one could be indifferent. But, he says, this sort of indifference would rely on taking recurrence as a cosmological thesis. As a psychological thesis, he says, only the reactions of despair or exhilaration are appropriate. "If my life were to recur, then it could recur only in identical fashion", because if there were any differences, it would not be my life. And with this realization, he says, we cannot remain indifferent (*Nietzsche*, 153).

But that does not escape Lucretius's Key. How should we react, once we understand that the myth, even if it were true, would be a description of something that could never change our experiences? Instead of falling into despair, or else shouting with joy, ought we not to say that the very thought is a thought of something that cannot make any difference, and so it is after all of no use? Like death itself, the myth ought to be "nothing to us".

Perhaps the myth could encourage a non-teleological attitude towards the unfolding of the world. Some people, faced with the idea of eternal recurrence, could be struck with the thought that *there is no point* to existence if existence merely repeats and does not progress towards a final goal. Just so. They have seen what Nietzsche wished to give them:

> Let us think this thought in its most terrible form: existence as it is, without meaning or aim, yet recurring inevitably without any finale of nothingness: "*the eternal recurrence*."

> This is the most extreme form of nihilism: the nothing (the "meaningless"), eternally!

> The European form of Buddhism: the energy of knowledge and strength compels this belief. It is the most *scientific* of all possible hypotheses. We deny end goals: if existence had one it would have to have been reached. [*Will to Power*, §55]

But a non-teleological attitude could be encouraged without resorting to an impossible myth. Suppose there are cycles, but each one is different. Or else suppose that there are no cycles; there is only a straight continuation. In either case one might be tempted to say "My life *will* (or at least can) make a difference". But one could also immediately ask "*So what?* Even if I now *hope* that what I do now could make a difference—perhaps even a great difference—in the future *beyond my present life*, I will never be able to know and experience the difference, and so I cannot reach that 'eternal confirmation and seal'. Postmortem differences cannot possibly make a difference to me—that is (to speak redundantly), to me in my life." Just so. This is now not a Nietzschean, but rather an Epicurean attitude.

It might be feared that such an attitude does not overcome the threat of nihilism which can arise in the face of an ultimately meaningless existence. But I could be filled with a terror of nihilism only if I already yearned for a point or purpose for the whole. But why would I want such a thing? The realization that there is for me eternal nothingness beyond my death ought not to fill me with terror, but rather ought to lead me to appreciate that fact as being absolutely nothing to me. Terror can arise only in connection with what I believe can matter to me. But what cannot possibly influence me should be understood as *not* mattering to me. Hence, eternal recurrence and eternal pointlessness of any sort should be nothing to me.

CLONING

One of the reasons why ontological issues of personal identity may seem puzzling is because they are sometimes presented by first postulating what can easily be conceived of as two persons and then asking how it is that they can be the same. Here, for example, is a comment by Jennifer Whiting: "Most of us believe that we have reason to care about our own future selves" ("Friends and Future Selves", 547). But do we really think we have "future selves"? This is a most awkward expression of a common conception. I believe that I have reason to care about myself and to take care what I will be and do. But I do not ever think of myself as having a "future self", because that term makes me think of a person different from, or at least other than, myself. My "future self" is (will be?) somewhat like my child, or my grandchild—some person who will issue from me somehow, but who not only is not me, but will not ever be me.

The idea of a "future self" being thought of (even if only implicitly) as other than myself is reinforced by Whiting when she contrasts caring for our "future selves" with caring for other persons. Apparently there is a problem: why should I care for my "future self" in some way different from how I care for other people? Further reinforcement of the feeling that there are two selves is given by talking of one's "future self" in the third person:

> It is supposed to be obvious that I have special reasons to
> care about my future self if she has my immaterial soul in a
> way in which it is not obvious that I have special reasons to
> care about her if all she is is someone whose experiences are
> connected in certain ways to my present ones. ["Friends and
> Future Selves," 547]

Martin Gough says something similar:

> The relation of egoism to Personal Identity lies in the fact
> that an identity relation must hold between a person in the
> present and a person in the future as a necessary condition of
> the person in the present acting in the interest of the person
> in the future and at the same time being egoistic. ["The
> Incoherence of Egoism", 2] [13]

Thus does one version of the problem of "personal identity" get started:
here (or now) is one person, and there (or then) is what appears to be another,
and we are to wonder whether there are any good reasons for claiming that they
are the same person. This is hard to do when the initial presumption gives us the
appearance of two persons. What matters to me is that *I* exist, not that "someone"
exists in the future, no matter how materially or psychologically "connected"
with me that "someone" might be. It is not some future self I am worried about;
it is *me*. If I am concerned about my well-being, then I am concerned about
me. If I want to be happy or to survive, I want *me*—"this person", to express it
awkwardly in a quasi-third-person form—to be happy or to survive.

This brings us to the issue of cloning. By "cloning" we usually mean
making a physical copy of an original. Would the physical part include a mind?
Lucretius would have thought so (in the case of humans, anyway), because he
thought of persons as bodies and souls "compacted into one whole" (3.838–839
and 3.845–846). Some recent writers try to make use of computer metaphors:
the hardware corresponds to the body and brain, and the software corresponds
to the mind. If "software" is understood abstractly, then programs and data
could be copied exactly from one machine to another. If we apply the metaphor
to persons, then we can imagine that a person's mind could be copied into
another body.[14]

Imagine being given a chance to be cloned. There you are, a normal
human being, but you are facing imminent death, and someone tells you (let
us suppose they are convincing about this) that your body can be cloned, and
a copy of your "mind" can be "downloaded" to the clone. Would you take the
opportunity? I think that most thoughtful people would hesitate.[15] They would

---

13 Other useful examples, chosen almost at random, are Zemach ("Looking Out
for Number One") and Parfit (*Reasons and Persons*, chapter 15). There are many,
many more.

14 This also means that two or more instances of the same mind could exist
simultaneously. If there were a way to make identical bodies and "download" the
same mind to all of them, it would be conceivable that the population of an entire
planet could be just multiple instances of the same person.

15 I said "let us suppose they are convincing about this". But can we, now, have much

hesitate because it would seem to them that the future clone would not be *them*, but rather a different "self"—in fact, merely a copy. Probably you would want survival not in the form of a different person, even if that different person were a perfect duplicate, because that would still leave you dead.

Even though the result of a cloning process is two persons, we might be able to appreciate how each could come to have a feeling of being so strongly connected with the other that some feelings of identity would arise. For me, the movie *The 6th Day* (directed by Roger Spottiswoode) made the idea of being cloned a little less problematic than it had been before. In this movie, the good guy, Adam Gibson (Arnold Schwarzenegger), has been cloned (by a very rapid cloning process), and he is being chased by bad guys who are also clones. The bad guys are no match for Adam, who manages to kill each of them. But they are subsequently re-cloned and then killed again. And again. At one point Adam mutters to one of them "Try to stay dead this time". The bad guys know that they are clones (of clones, etc.). One bad guy is cloned after having been run over by a car, and he complains about the pain in his chest where the car ran over him. Later on he is killed by having his neck snapped; the clone wakes up complaining about the pain where his neck was broken. Another bad guy clone dismisses such complaints: "We've all been killed before".

Apparently these clones have no problem identifying themselves as continuations of earlier selves. Even the main bad guy Drucker (Tony Goldwyn), dying from a gunshot wound with only moments to live, tries desperately to start up the cloning machine in order to create a clone of himself, presumably in an effort to survive death, which he believes he has done before, because he himself is a clone.

In your ordinary life you are willing to say that your present experiences are (of course) continuous with your memories—they seem to form a unified whole which is your psychic history. But if you are now given convincing proof that you are a clone of a former person, you might be more cautious in what you say; you might say that what *seem* to be your memories *seem* to form a continuous whole. Suppose you discover that your former self was killed, but a "recording" of your "mind" (your former self's "mind") was made just before death, and a new physical clone was grown (very quickly) and your "mind" (your former self's "mind") "downloaded" into the clone, which woke up believing that it was you. From the point of view of you-as-the-clone, you woke up believing that you were of course you.

Now suppose you are (again) killed and your "mind" "downloaded" into yet another clone. Imagine waking up as this new clone. You would have all the older memories (or at least they would *seem* to be yours). Suppose you also

confidence that we could accurately anticipate how we would react if we were convinced that there were such things as minds that could be transferred to other organisms?

know about the cloning. Perhaps you could be—and could know that you were—actually a clone of a clone (of a clone …); perhaps death and re-existence would seem to you to have occurred a number of times before. It is quite plausible that, in spite of my description of the affair as one of originals and copies, you would come to acknowledge and to rely on what seem to be your experiences of being continuous with all the former "selves", and the whole business of continuation via cloning might seem to be such a normal occurrence that no philosophical puzzle about identity would disturb you.

If, for example, you were faced with a life-threatening disease and had the chance to be cloned again, you might unhesitatingly agree to it. You might think "*I* remember having been cloned many times before, and yet here *I* still am, continuing. So being cloned is a convenient way of *my* continuing." It is possible, therefore, that a clone could have a strong sense of having continued across what to an external observer might seem to be multiple persons. For many people, all that is necessary to ensure identity through change is psychological continuity. Could cloning, then, be a satisfactory way of surviving annihilation? Could it be that survival as a copy could have the necessary internal evidence to support it?

There is no present reason to think so, and that is because we have been imagining that a clone could somehow be given the original's "mind" (especially the memories). But so far, anyway, that possibility is both technologically and philosophically without secure foundation. If we discard the magic of mind transfer, then a clone is *merely* a copy. Even if you discovered convincing evidence that you were a clone, that fact would be of no relevance to the issue of whether you could survive your eventual death, unless you also had appropriate memories which would constitute internal evidence of some kind of prior life.

CONCLUSION

There is good reason to reject the rebirth (transmigration) hypothesis. The only external evidence is the occasional claim that someone (such as Gautama Buddha) remembered one or more past lives. But that kind of evidence is also consistent with the falsity of the hypothesis. And given that we have no internal evidence (i.e., appropriate memories), the hypothesis ought to be dismissed as doing no work.

The hypothesis of recurrence, at least in Nietzsche's dramatic, universal version, fares no better. A perfectly repeated world cannot be distinguished from a non-repeated world, and so upon examination the hypothesis is idle.

Unlike eternal recurrence, if cloning or recombination did happen, then there *could* be both internal and external evidence for it. But as a matter of fact, we presently have no internal or external evidence of continuation via cloning, just as we have no internal or external evidence of continuation via a perfect recombination of our atoms.

It seems therefore that it is unlikely that anyone who was interested in avoiding annihilation could be content with any of the hypotheses here discussed. On the other hand, if we understood death correctly—i.e., as Epicurus and Lucretius advise—then the fact that our lives will eventually reach a conclusion would be nothing to us.[16]

SELECT BIBLIOGRAPHY

Alderman, Harold. *Nietzsche's Gift*. Athens, Ohio: Ohio University Press, 1977.

Epicurus. *Letter to Menoeceus*. In *Lives of the Eminent Philosophers*, by Diogenes Laertius, vol. 2, bk. 10. Translated by R. D. Hicks. Cambridge, Mass.: Harvard University Press, Loeb Classical Library, 1931.

———. *Letter to Pythocles*. In *Lives of the Eminent Philosophers*, by Diogenes Laertius, vol. 2, bk. 10. Translated by R. D. Hicks. Cambridge, Mass.: Harvard University Press, Loeb Classical Library, 1931.

Gough, Martin. "The Incoherence of Egoism", *Philosophical Papers* 27 (1998): 1–28.

Kaufmann, Walter. *Nietzsche: Philosopher, Psychologist, Antichrist*, 4th ed. Princeton: Princeton University Press, 1974.

Lucretius. *De Rerum Natura*. Translated by W. H. D. Rouse and Martin F. Smith. Cambridge, Mass.: Harvard University Press, Loeb Classical Library, 1992.

Nehamas, Alexander. *Nietzsche: Life as Literature*. Cambridge, Mass.: Harvard University Press, 1985.

Nietzsche, Friedrich. *Beyond Good and Evil*. In *Basic Writings of Nietzsche*, edited and translated by Walter Kaufmann. New York: The Modern Library, 1992.

———. *The Gay Science*. In *The Portable Nietzsche*, edited and translated by Walter Kaufmann. New York: Penguin Books, 1976.

———. "Why I am So Clever". In *Ecce Homo*. In *Basic Writings of Nietzsche*, edited and translated by Walter Kaufmann. New York: The Modern Library, 1992.

16 Thanks to Christine Sage Suits for her comments on an early draft of this paper.

―――. *The Will to Power*. Translated by Walter Kaufmann and R. J. Hollingdale. New York: Vintage, 1968.

Parfit, Derek. *Reasons and Persons*. New York: Oxford University Press, 1984.

Spottiswoode, Roger, et al. *The 6th Day*. Phoenix Pictures, 2000.

Wadia, A. R. "Philosophical Implications of the Doctrine of Karma". *Philosophy East and West* 15 (1965): 145–152.

Warren, James. "Lucretian *Palingenesis* Recycled". *Classical Quarterly* 51 (2001): 499–508.

Whiting, Jennifer. "Friends and Future Selves". *Philosophical Review* 95 (1986): 547–580.

Zemach, Eddy M. "Looking Out for Number One". *Philosophy and Phenomenological Research* 48 (1987): 209–233.

Z

Zaehner, R. C., 111
Zemach, Eddy M., 128
Zeno, 34
Zoroaster, 30

Vincent Bissonette (Ph.D., CUNY) has written on the passion of anger as it figures in philosophical and poetic texts from Hobbes to Coleridge, and has published on the poetry of Coleridge and Dryden. He teaches English at Allendale Columbia School in Rochester, N.Y.

Dane R. Gordon is Emeritus Professor of Philosophy at Rochester Institute of Technology. Some of his books include: *A Feeling Intellect and A Thinking Heart*; *Philosophy and Vision*; *The Old Testament in its Cultural, Historical and Religious Context*; and *Thinking and Reading in Philosophy of Religion*. His most recent publications are *St. Petersburg: Poems*, and *The Logic of Death: Poems of War*.

William B. Jensen is Oesper Professor of Chemical Education and History of Chemistry at the University of Cincinnati. The author of over 170 papers, reviews and books in the fields of inorganic chemistry, chemical education, and history of chemistry, Dr. Jensen is also a Past Chair of the ACS Division of the History of Chemistry, the founding editor of the *Bulletin for the History of Chemistry*, and recipient of the Division's 2005 Edelstein Award for Outstanding Achievement in the History of Chemistry.

John R. Lenz is Associate Professor and Chair of Classics at Drew University in Madison, New Jersey. He received his Ph.D. in Classical Studies from Columbia University, was a Fulbright scholar in Greece, and has also taught at Columbia, Union College, and Texas A&M University. He served as President of the Bertrand Russell Society from 1994–1998.

Timothy J. Madigan is Assistant Professor of Philosophy at St. John Fisher College. He is a U.S. Editor of *Philosophy Now* and the author of *W.K. Clifford and "The Ethics of Belief"*.

John R. A. Mayer is Professor Emeritus of Philosophy at Brock University, in St. Catharines, Ontario, Canada. Prior to being the founding chair of Philosophy at Brock, he taught at McMaster University, in Hamilton, and completed his Ph.D. at Emory University. He is also an active Unitarian, and an activist on a variety of social issues.

Charles M. Natoli is Professor and Chair, Department of Philosophy and Classical Studies, St. John Fisher College. He is the author of *Fire in the Dark: Essays on the Pensées and Provinciales of Pascal*.

Melissa M. Shew teaches at Marquette University, where she works in both the history of philosophy and contemporary Continental philosophy. She completed her dissertation in Ancient Greek philosophy at the University of Oregon (2008).

David B. Suits is professor of Philosophy at Rochester Institute of Technology. Among his research interests are Epicureanism, anarchism, and the philosophy of mind.

COLOPHON

DESIGN	Bruce Meader
PRODUCTION	Marnie Soom
TYPEFACE	Adobe Minion Pro
PRINTING	Lightning Source USA

CPSIA information can be obtained at www.ICGtesting.com
Printed in the USA
BVOW05s2201030814

361131BV00001B/41/P